The
HEARTBEAT
Chronicles

The
HEARTBEAT
Chronicles

The life and times of Aidensfield
through the pages of

The Ashfordly Gazette

GRANADA MEDIA **Companion to the ITV series**   **Geoff Tibballs**

First published in Great Britain in 1999 by Granada Media

an imprint of André Deutsch Limited
in association with Granada Media Group
76 Dean Street
London W1V 5HA
www.vci.co.uk

2 4 6 8 10 9 7 5 3 1

A catalogue record for this book is available from the British Library

ISBN 0 233 99724 5

Editorial and Design by Design/Section

Printed in the UK by Butler and Tanner, Frome and London

Contents

Introduction

At the tail end of last year a new broom arrived at Ashfordly Police Station. On the other end of it was a sergeant who ordered a thorough clear-out to make the place ready for tackling crime in the millennium. No stone was left unturned. Among the interesting finds were a cheese and pickle sandwich, believed to date from around 1966, and a collection of back copies of the Aidensfield edition of the *Ashfordly Gazette*. Discovered gathering dust in a little-used cupboard, they initially appeared to be nothing more than a pile of old newspapers, but so fascinating did they prove that even the sergeant temporarily abandoned the spring-cleaning session to leaf through the pages. They might not have had the historical impact of the Dead Sea Scrolls but they formed an invaluable chronicle of life in Aidensfield in the mid-1960s, a period of time recaptured by the hugely successful television series *Heartbeat*. The proprietors of the *Gazette* have generously given permission for selected pages from this archive material to be reproduced in book form.

Ashfordly Gazette

With which is incorporated the "Ashfordly Times and North Yorkshire Advertiser"

Registered at the General Post Office as a Newspaper   Established 1856 No. 5,645.   Printed and Published by HORNE & SON. LIMITED. WHITBY   FRIDAY, APRIL 10th, 1964.   12 Pages.   Price 3d.   Tel. 396 (Editorial Tel. 1070)

AIDENSFIELD EDITION

YOUTHS IN BRAWL AT VILLAGE DANCE

A gang of scooter-riding youths terrorised local teenagers at a dance at Aidensfield Village Hall on Saturday night. The trouble-makers, believed to have come from Ashfordly, smashed bottles and wrecked the sound equipment of the pop group The Telstars who were performing at the dance. After fighting broke out, one man was arrested. He will appear in court next week.

As frightened youngsters fled the dance, further trouble was prevented by the swift intervention of Aidensfield's new village constable, P.C. Nick Rowan.

He told the *Gazette*: 'We'd had a tip-off that kids from Ashfordly were looking for revenge on local bikers following the clashes at Clacton on Easter Monday.'

The tearaways, who like to be called 'Mods' because of their preference for smart clothes and who are the sworn enemies of scruffy leather-jacketed motorcyclists known as 'Rockers', had earlier extinguished the famous Aidensfield Arms fire. The fire, which had been burning since 1860 to commemorate the night when Queen Victoria took shelter at the inn after being caught in a storm, was put out when the gang urinated on it.

Landlord George Ward raged: 'It was sheer vandalism. They want locking up, the lot of them.' The fire has since been rebuilt.

The Telstars get the youngsters 'dancing on a Saturday night'.

VILLAGE GETS NEW P.C.

As mentioned elsewhere on this page, Aidensfield has a new policeman. He is Constable Nick Rowan, 26, who has been transferred from the Metropolitan Police in London. He is joined by his doctor wife, Kate, who is not quite a stranger to the area, having been born in Eltering. The couple have been married for three years. They do not have children.

BUDGIE CHARGE THROWN OUT

Aidensfield man Claude Jeremiah Greengrass, 58, was acquitted at Ashfordly Magistrates' Court on Tuesday of a charge that his dog had worried livestock on agricultural land.

Conducting his own defence, Mr. Greengrass admitted that his lurcher dog, Alfred, had entered a breeding aviary at North End Farm, Aidensfield, last month and killed a budgerigar. But he protested that a budgerigar does not constitute livestock and that an aviary is not legally classed as agricultural land.

After consulting the Dogs (Protection of Livestock) Act 1953, the magistrates agreed with the defendant and acquitted him of the charge.

A jubilant Mr. Greengrass said afterwards: 'This is a victory for justice.'

Sgt. Oscar Blaketon of Ashfordly Police declined to comment.

BRIGADE FIGHT BARN FIRE

— Arson Suspected

Aidensfield's newest P.C., Nick Rowan, questions farmer Jack Potter and his wife.

Ashfordly firemen fought for two hours to bring a barn fire near Aidensfield under control on Tuesday night. As firemen sprayed their hoses over the burning hay, police officers and local farmers managed to lead horses and cattle to safety before the beams of the barn finally gave way. Damage is estimated at over £100.

The distraught barn owner — Mrs. Helen Briggsby — reported hearing the sound of a motorcycle shortly before the fire started, leading the police to suspect that the fire may have been started deliberately.

CLUES ASK QUESTIONS

Motorcycle tyre tracks were discovered outside the barn and a woman's necklace was found inside.

This is the second suspicious barn fire in the area in the short space of only six weeks. A motorcycle was also heard roaring off on the previous occasion, at Elsinby. Sgt. Oscar Blaketon of Ashfordly Police commented: 'There's too much arson about round here for my liking.'

'BUS FLASHER' EXPOSED

An unsavoury incident was reported to the police on Thursday last after a passenger had allegedly exposed himself to the conductress on the Aidensfield bus.

The conductress in question, Hannah Davies, said that an unkempt man in a raincoat boarded the bus at Kirby Moor. As she went to collect his fare, she claimed that he pulled back his raincoat to reveal his manhood. She screamed and the man immediately fled from the moving vehicle.

STUMPED

The culprit was revealed to be local farmer Jack Potter … an amputee whose arm ends in a rounded stump. It was the stump which Miss Davies had seen beneath his raincoat before jumping to the wrong conclusion.

'It was simply a case of mistaken identity,' said P.C. Nick Rowan.

POACHED SALMON — LOCAL OFFICERS MISS THE CATCH

Poachers struck on Lord Ashfordly's estate this week, stealing his most valuable salmon stock. At the time of the theft, police officers from Ashfordly were staking out a stretch of water further along the river.

His Lordship raged: 'While the police were sitting on their backsides, the buggers were emptying my best pool. It's ruined my fishing for the rest of the season.'

Two men from York were being interviewed last night. As a result of salmon recovered from a christening at the Aidensfield Arms, a local man, Claude Jeremiah Greengrass, 60, was also helping police with their enquiries.

GUN DRAMA
AT REMOTE FARM

— Shots Fired At Police

The rural tranquility of Aidensfield was shattered this week by a shotgun siege which left Callanrigg Farm looking more like the Ponderosa from the popular television series *Bonanza*.

The drama began on Wednesday morning when Mrs. Mary Radcliffe, who lives two miles from Callanrigg, reported her husband missing. Her call prompted P.C. Nick Rowan to search Callanrigg, home of farmer Matthew Chapman, a Scot in his mid-forties.

DOUBLE KIDNAP

There, P.C. Rowan found Dick Radcliffe huddled in a corner in an upstairs room. The room had been stripped bare apart from a camp bed. Mr. Radcliffe, a diabetic, was in such a bad way that he was barely able to speak to the young officer.

When P.C. Rowan tried to summon help, he was confronted in the doorway by Chapman, brandishing a shotgun. The Constable was then locked in the room with the ailing Mr. Radcliffe.

'It was quite frightening,' admitted P.C. Rowan. 'By the evening Mr. Radcliffe had lapsed into a state of unconsciousness so I knew I had to obtain medical assistance somehow.

DARING ESCAPE

'I found a collection of war comics and slid one under the door. I then tore off a strip of paper and forced it into the key hole. It pushed out the key which fell on to the comic. I then carefully pulled the comic back under the door so that I could reach the key.'

(continued on page 6)

Farmer Matthew Chapman (left) confronts Dick Radcliffe over an affair of the heart — and an attack on his farm.

ARSON CHARGE

A 21-year-old Manningby man, named as Ian Clayton of Esk Road, has been charged in connection with a barn fire at Helen Briggsby's farm last week. He has also been charged with deliberately starting a fire at Elsinby in March.

THE WORLD ABOUT US

- Twelve members of the Great Train Robbery gang have been sentenced to a total of 307 years in jail.

- The Queen has named her new son Edward.

- British businessman Greville Wynne, jailed as a spy by the Russians, was freed by Moscow in exchange for KGB agent Gordon Lonsdale.

- A new television channel, BBC2, opened this week. But first night programmes were blacked out by a power cut.

POLICE SEEK TIDY THIEF

Ashfordly Police were this week hunting a silverware burglar who has taken to tidying up after breaking into houses.

At Strensford vicarage the thief put away some plates; at a house in Elsinby he did the washing up; and at a burglary in Ashfordly he tidied away a pile of magazines.

On Monday night he struck again, this time in Aidensfield. He made off with two silver candlesticks from a house on Moor Lane ... but only after completing a jigsaw puzzle which had been left unfinished on the living room table.

'It's certainly an unusual case,' admitted Sgt. Oscar Blaketon. 'We're used to burglars making a mess, but I've never come across one who is house-proud!'

P.C. Alfred Ventress pictured with two hard-boiled eggs, similar to the one he dropped in the siege.

GUN DRAMA
(continued from page 2)

Escaping from his imprisonment, P.C. Rowan was able to alert fellow officers at Ashfordly. But as the patrol car approached Callanrigg, Chapman suddenly emerged from the farmhouse and fired at the vehicle, forcing it to swerve. One shot cracked a side window of the car, narrowly missing its occupants, Sgt. Oscar Blaketon, P.C. Alfred Ventress and Dr. Kate Rowan.

The shock made P.C. Ventress drop a hard-boiled egg which he was eating at the time.

WIFE STEPS IN

In an attempt to resolve the situation peacefully, the police brought Mrs. Radcliffe forward to talk with Chapman. When this failed, Chapman turned the gun on himself. But before he could pull the trigger, P.C. Rowan managed to disarm him. Neither man was injured.

With speculation mounting as to what caused Chapman to incarcerate Mr. Radcliffe, it emerged that Chapman and Mrs. Radcliffe — or Mary Patterson as she was then — had been betrothed 20 years ago. When Chapman failed to return from the war, Miss Patterson had assumed that he was dead. So she married Mr. Radcliffe instead.

Chapman had harboured a grudge against his love rival ever since. He thought Mr. Radcliffe was responsible for an attack on his property although the police confirmed yesterday that this was the work of local schoolboys.

Mr. Radcliffe was recovering in Whitby Hospital last night. Charges are expected to be preferred against Chapman.

CORRECTION

The contribution of the Misses Simpkins at the Aidensfield Handicrafts Fair was smocking and rugs and not smoking drugs, as was stated in last week's *Gazette*.

PROTEST CANCELLED AS SPEAKER TAKEN ILL

A 'Ban The Bomb' protest planned to take place at the Fylingdales early warning station on Saturday was cancelled at the last minute when the principal speaker was struck down with illness.

The demonstration at the American-run centre on the outskirts of Aidensfield was expected to attract large crowds of long-haired protesters from as far afield as Scarborough.

Hundreds had already converged on Lord Ashfordly's land, erecting tents, drinking bottles of shandy and listening to loud pop music. Some were reportedly tuning in to illegal pirate radio stations such as Radio Caroline which began broadcasting off the east coast in March.

But no sooner had the guest speaker, prospective Parliamentary candidate Paul Melthorn, begun his rallying call than he was taken ill.

Doctors diagnosed that he was suffering from heartburn. The protesters, who had earlier been involved in clashes with workers at the station, drifted away quietly, allaying fears of Ashfordly Police that the 'invasion' would get out of hand.

MELTHORN'S MISERY

The cancellation marked the end of an unhappy two days for Mr. Melthorn. The previous night he had literally been caught with his trousers down when robbed of his wallet at knifepoint while discussing strategy with one of his female supporters in her tent.

A suspect was later pursued on motorcycle across the moors but, riding back towards the demonstrators, he was brought to ground by a blow from a 'Ban The Bomb' placard wielded by Dr. Kate Rowan. Two men are due to appear in court next week in connection with the robbery.

Protestors at Ashfordly train station, prior to clashes with workers.

DOCTOR JOINS PRACTICE

Aidensfield G.P. Dr. Alex Ferrenby announced this week that Dr. Kate Rowan has become a partner in his practice. Dr. Rowan has lived in Aidensfield for four months. Her husband is village Constable Nick Rowan.

THE WORLD ABOUT US

– Ian Fleming, creator of James Bond, died last week of a heart attack. He was 56.

– Great Train Robber Charlie Wilson is on the run after escaping from jail.

– Beat group Manfred Mann top the popular hit parade with 'Do Wah Diddy Diddy'.

– The BBC have announced the introduction of a new football programme, *Match of the Day*.

FARMER'S SON CHARGED WITH CHURCH THEFT

— *Circus man released*

The son of a local farmer was yesterday charged with the theft of the cash box from Aidensfield Church. 23-year-old Jamie Hunter was arrested following a police raid on his father's farm on the outskirts of Aidensfield.

The cash box containing £50 was stolen from the church on Sunday night. The collection box was also rifled and a small amount of damage was done to the interior of the church.

RED 'RAG' TO THE POLICE

The discovery of a red handkerchief at the scene of the crime led officers to suspect Milos Lazlos, a member of a family of travelling circus performers whose presence in the village has aroused considerable hostility. On Saturday Mr. Lazlos and Hunter had been involved in a fracas at Aidensfield Stores. The Lazlos family dog was seen escaping with a string of sausages.

But when a local man, Claude Jeremiah Greengrass, 56, came forward and told officers that Mr. Lazlos had been out poaching with him on the night of the church theft, the investigation switched elsewhere.

It is thought that Hunter had tried to incriminate Mr. Lazlos after the two had had a falling out over the daughter of the vicar, Anna Collingsworth.

A tight-lipped Sgt. Oscar Blaketon of Ashfordly Police

Farmer Hunter (left, foreground) and Milos Lazlos (right) are prevented from fighting by son and mother, respectively.

said: 'We are of course extremely grateful to Mr. Greengrass for showing us the error of our ways. My only regret is that since there has been no complaint about his poaching activities, we are unable to prosecute him.'

But I have every confidence that his time will come.' Mr. Greengrass only commented: 'That's slander, is that.'

ORGANIST SACKED

Mr. Hector Whitcombe, organist at St. Mark's, Elsinby, was relieved of his duties this week after a mix-up over sheet music caused him to play 'I've Got a Lovely Bunch of Coconuts' at a funeral. A member of the deceased's family said: 'It's about time he went. He doesn't know his arias from his Elgar'.

THE WORLD ABOUT US

– Long jumpers Lynn Davies and Mary Rand and 800 metres runner Ann Packer won gold for Britain at the Tokyo Olympics.

– New Prime Minister Harold Wilson warned of an impending economic crisis.

– Ian Smith, Prime Minister of Southern Rhodesia, sent Britain an ultimatum regarding his country's desire for independence.

Ashfordly Gazette

With which is incorporated the "Ashfordly Times and North Yorkshire Advertiser"

Registered at the General Post Office as a Newspaper | Established 1856 No. 5675. | Printed and Published by HORNE & SON. LIMITED. WHITBY | FRIDAY, NOVEMBER 6th, 1964. | 12 Pages. | Price 3d. | Tel. 396 (Editorial Tel. 1070)

AIDENSFIELD EDITION

MOTHER-IN-LAW GETS LIFE SENTENCE FOR GUN MURDER

— Local Community Shaken By Octogenarian Killing Of Ex-Policeman

Eighty-two-year-old Mrs. Victoria Wainwright was sentenced to life imprisonment at York Assizes on Wednesday for the murder of her son-in-law, retired police officer Andrew Gerard.

Mr. Gerard, who had risen to the rank of Detective Chief Superintendent with the Metropolitan Police, was found dead at his home at Penketh House, Aidensfield, in July. He had been shot twice.

34 YEARS OF UNHAPPY DAYS

The court heard how Mrs. Wainwright, who lived at Penketh House with Mr. Gerard and his wife Muriel, had carefully plotted the murder in revenge for her son-in-law's cruelty.

Although the Gerards had been married for 34 years and appeared outwardly happy, Mr. Gerard was prone to extremely violent

Mrs Victoria Wainwright (left) and her daughter.

mood swings. Mrs. Gerard had once told local GP Dr. Alex Ferrenby that her husband had given her a black eye during a heated argument that they had. She lived in such fear of being hit again that she had to take tranquilisers to calm her nerves.

On the morning of Sunday 12 July, concealing her late husband's old army revolver about her person, Mrs. Wainwright went to church early to arrange the flowers. She was seen there by the verger, Mr. Roland Shaw, thus providing her with what seemed originally like a watertight alibi.

VERGER FOOLED — BUT NOT POLICE

But when the verger went up into the tower to ring the bells, Mrs. Wainwright was able to take a crafty short-cut back to the house and shoot Mr. Gerard as he stood alone by one of the downstairs windows.

By that time, Mr. Gerard was alone in the house, his wife having followed her mother on to church.

The sound of the bells was easily loud enough to drown out the din of gunfire.

(continued on page 7)

THE WORLD ABOUT US

- London's Windmill Theatre announced that it is closing for good.

- Lyndon B. Johnson was re-elected President of the United States.

- Bare-footed singer Sandie Shaw enjoyed a second week at the top of the hit parade with 'Always Something There To Remind Me'.

- ITV launched a new afternoon serial, *Crossroads*.

MURDER TRIAL

(continued from page 1)

Mrs. Wainwright then slipped back to church before the service began without anybody having missed her.

When she and her daughter returned home at noon, they found the body of Mr. Gerard.

Officers from Scotland Yard were drafted in from London as police began to fear that the deceased might have been the victim of a grudge killing. Photographs of four recently-released criminals who had been 'put away' by Mr. Gerard were circulated among the villagers of Aidensfield but failed to elicit a response.

CONFESSION HELPS THE BOYS IN BLUE

After the officer in charge of the case, Detective Chief Inspector Pat Merton, had continued to tell reporters that he thought the murder was the work of a professional, police suddenly arrested Mrs. Gerard. Apparently, it was seeing her only daughter being taken away by the authorities that prompted Mrs. Wainwright to confess to Aidensfield's P.C. Nick Rowan.

P.C. Rowan told the court: 'Late on the afternoon of Friday 17 July, my wife and I were walking along the path at the rear of the church. I had seen the path from the top of the church tower and knew that it led to Penketh House via the churchyard. I also knew that Mrs. Wainwright used the path regularly to tend the grave of her late husband.

MOTHER'S GRIEF

'It occurred to me that she could have used it on the day of the murder without being seen. At that point, Mrs. Wainwright emerged from the house and engaged me in conversation. She was upset because her daughter had been arrested. I told her: 'I don't think she did it ... so that just leaves you.' To my surprise, she made no attempt to deny the accusation and proceeded to pour out her heart.'

Mrs. Wainwright, who pleaded guilty to the killing, said in her statement: 'I was the only thing that stood between my daughter and her husband — his constant bullying and violent tempers. He had spent too many years dealing with criminals. He treated us with the same contempt.

'And when he finally hit her, I couldn't stand it any longer. But he told me if I interfered, he would put me in a home. What else could I do to save my daughter? After all it is the most primal instinct for a mother to protect her young.'

LENIENT JUDGE ALLOWS WIDOW TO LIVE

After the shooting, she said she had kept the revolver hidden in her late husband's grave.

Exercising clemency, Judge Norman Phillips decided that the death penalty would be inappropriate in this case. It comes as no great surprise because next month MPs are expected to vote in favour of the abolition of capital punishment.

Mrs Wainwright (background, left) and her ex-son-in-law (bottom of picture).

We apologise to readers who entered last week's Spot the Difference competition. Due to a printing error, instead of two similar drawings of York Minster, we published one of the Minster and one of the Rt. Hon. Barbara Castle, MP. Sorry to all those readers who wrote in pointing out as many as 267 differences between the two.

LOCAL MAN FINED FOR SHEEP RUSTLING

Farmer Alec Huggett, 67, talks to Constable Nick Rowan about his missing sheep.

— Tried To Pull Wool Over Magistrates' Eyes

Aidensfield resident Claude Jeremiah Greengrass was fined £100 at Ashfordly Magistrates' Court on Tuesday after being convicted of sheep rustling.

Greengrass, 64, was found to be a member of a gang which stole six ewes in a night raid on the farm of Mr. Alec Huggett. Mr. Huggett recognised his sheep when Greengrass later tried to sell them at the Livestock Mart in Ashfordly.

The magistrates heard how Mr. Huggett knew each member of his flock individually by their distinguishing marks. Greengrass protested that he had bought the animals in good faith.

After sentencing, Greengrass, whose five previous court appearances had seen him acquitted on each occasion, accused the police — and Sgt. Oscar Blaketon in particular — of harassment. 'I'm an honest man, but I've been hounded,' he claimed.

A jubilant Sgt. Blaketon proclaimed it a proud day for Ashfordly Police. 'It's taken us a long time to get a conviction against Greengrass. I only wish it was 100 years ago when they still had hanging for sheep rustling!'

WHAT'S ON
. . . .

Saturday. Whitby Essoldo. The Searchers. Doors Open 7.30pm. Tickets 8s 6d.

Saturday. Church Hall, Aidensfield. Ashfordly & District Cigarette Card Society Exhibition. 2pm. Entrance Free.

Saturday–Friday. Whitby Gaumont. *Mary Poppins*. 3.15pm, 7.30pm. Tickets From 3s 9d. (Children 2s 0d).

Saturday–Friday. Ashfordly Regal. *A Hard Day's Night*. 3.30pm, 7pm. Tickets From 3s 6d. (Children 1s 9d).

Monday. St. Peter's Church Hall. Whitby Trawlermen's Association Talk: 'Cod Moves In Mysterious Ways'. 7.30pm.

Tuesday. Aidensfield Village Hall. Ladies' Fashion Show – All The Latest Crimplene Designs. 7.30pm. Admission 1s 6d.

Wednesday. Aidensfield Village Hall. Ashfordly Townswomen's Guild Debate: Is 'Ready, Steady Go!' A Corrupting Influence? 2pm. Coffee 6d.

Thursday. The slide show and talk on Crime Prevention due to have been given by P.C. Phil Bellamy at Ashfordly Town Hall has had to be cancelled because the projector has been stolen.

LORD ASHFORDLY'S CHAUFFEUR CHARGED WITH SHOE ROBBERY

— Arrest Follows Much Sole Searching And Pounding The Beat

Twenty-eight-year-old Michael Lewis, chauffeur to Lord Ashfordly for the past three months, has been charged with robbery following a shotgun ambush on Elsinby Moor last Friday.

P.C. INJURED

Officers from Ashfordly Police Station raided Ashfordly Hall on Monday evening and arrested Lewis after a scuffle. P.C. Nick Rowan, who seized Lewis as he tried to make his escape, was treated for minor cuts and bruises.

The police took away a holdall containing a wad of money, a pair of ladies' high-heeled shoes and a pair of Lord Ashfordly's valuable candlesticks.

The armed robbery had taken place on a quiet spot on the moor at 7.45 last Friday evening. Joe Duffy, well-known proprietor of Duffy's Boots and Shoes on Ashfordly Market, had got out of his van to unlock a gate when he was confronted by a masked man dressed all in black and armed with a shotgun.

STRIP AND RUN

The robber snatched a bodypouch containing an undisclosed sum of money from Mr. Duffy's waist and forced him to strip to his shoes. As if that were not humiliation enough, he then drove off in Mr. Duffy's van which contained the trader's entire stock of shoes, boots and slippers.

The crime was discovered when a passing cyclist, Miss Gertrude Eckersley, spotted the naked Mr. Duffy running across the moor. She was later said to be as well as expected.

(continued on page 8)

Joe Duffy — local shoeseller — without a stitch.

CORRECTION

The subject of the Misses Simpkins's address at the Aidensfield New Year Parade was 'Cake-Making & Baking' not 'Makin' Bacon', as was stated in last week's *Gazette*.

THE WORLD ABOUT US

- The state funeral of Winston Churchill took place at St. Paul's Cathedral in London.

- American civil rights leader Dr. Martin Luther King was arrested in Alabama.

- Australian runner Ron Clarke broke the world 5000 metres record for the second time in just over two weeks.

- American duo The Righteous Brothers beat Cilla Black to number one with their version of 'You've Lost That Lovin' Feelin''.

BIG BOOTY

(continued from page 2)

Apart from noting a Scottish accent, Mr. Duffy was unable to give any other clues as to the modern-day highwayman's identity.

SHOES APLENTY

Police immediately deduced that the culprit was a local man, not only because he appeared aware of Mr. Duffy's movements but also because items from his haul started to appear in the Aidensfield area. Dr. Kate Rowan was presented with a pair of pink fluffy slippers by a grateful patient and local entrepreneur Claude Jeremiah Greengrass, 61, was found in possession of a pair of stolen boots.

SMOKING REMAINS

As officers stepped up their search for the wandering footwear, they also looked into any reported thefts of shotguns in the district. Among the missing firearms was one from Ashfordly Hall.

On Sunday Mr. Duffy's van turned up in a derelict barn three miles from Ashfordly Hall. At the scene P.C. Rowan discovered a discarded cigarette-end from a smoker who rolls his own.

Noting that Lord Ashfordly's chauffeur favoured this method of tobacco inhalation, P.C. Rowan decided to look into the man's background. The name he used — Danny Pearce — was found to be an alias and the address he had given as his previous place of employment — the Royal Hotel in York — had never heard of him. Armed with this information, officers searched the man's room at Ashfordly Hall and arrested him.

TYING UP LOOSE ENDS

'It's a good result for us,' said Sgt. Oscar Blaketon of Ashfordly police. 'Let's just say Michael Lewis is not unknown to the Met.'

Lewis is expected to appear in court next week.

CHICKEN POX OUTBREAK WORRIES LOCAL PARENTS

Dr. Kate Rowan (right) reassures mum-to-be Danielle Tilley about the chicken pox outbreak.

Medical staff in Aidensfield are bracing themselves for an epidemic of chicken pox following a potentially serious number of reported cases among children in the village. The outbreak is thought to have originated at the first meeting of a mother and baby group organised by the recently appointed Dr. Kate Rowan. Dr. Rowan yesterday assured parents: 'There is no cause for alarm.'

SHEEP RUN AMOK AT VILLAGE FÊTE

Upwards of 100 sheep caused chaos in Aidensfield on Saturday afternoon when they escaped from the village's winter fête. Traffic was brought to a standstill, a hot roasted chestnuts tandem was overturned and an elderly cyclist was deposited in a ditch.

At the height of the unrest, publican George Ward was forced to eject a dozen sheep from the public bar of the Aidensfield Arms. 'They were definitely under-age,' he said later.

The march of militant mutton extended to the village store where assistant Mary Gibbs could only look on helplessly as the animals chewed lettuce leaves and made off with a packet of acid drop Spangles and a bag of aniseed balls from the sweet counter.

Appropriately the flock was eventually rounded up by Rev. Aubrey Collingsworth,

The woolly terrors that ruined Aidenfield's first outdoor fête for four years.

P.C. Nick Rowan in a somehow less familiar guise.

vicar of Aidensfield Church, with a little help from farmer George Squires, P.C. Nick Rowan and members of the Aidensfield Boy Scouts.

WEATHER-BEATEN

The sheep are thought to have escaped when the gate on their pen blew open. Ironically the unseasonably mild weather meant that it was the first time in four years that the winter fête has been able to be staged outdoors.

There was a minor altercation afterwards when local man Claude Jeremiah Greengrass, 53, claimed that his winning tombola ticket had been eaten by one of the sheep. Judges rejected his claim on the first prize.

Later Mr. Greengrass said he would appeal. Sgt. Oscar Blaketon of Ashfordly Police, deputy chairman of the fête committee, responded: 'He certainly doesn't appeal to me.'

THE WORLD ABOUT US

– Minister of Health Kenneth Robinson announced that cigarette advertising is to be banned from television.

– American planes attacked Communist Viet Cong bases in North Vietnam.

– Beatles drummer Ringo Starr married Liverpool hairdresser Maureen Cox.

DOCTOR TAKEN CAPTIVE BY CRAZED GUNMAN

— Ordeal For G.P. In Disused Tunnel

Dr. Rowan at the wheel of her own car, threatened at gunpoint by an old 'enemy' of her husband, P.C. Nick Rowan.

A idensfield doctor Kate Rowan was today recovering from a terrifying ordeal at the hands of a gunman who abducted her when she answered his call for help.

Dr. Rowan was driving along the Strensford road to visit a patient at around 3.45 on Saturday afternoon when she spotted a man apparently having an asthma attack on the grass verge. As she stopped to help, the man drew a revolver and forced her to drive to the sidings near Ashfordly station.

FORCED AT GUNPOINT

From there, he made her walk along an abandoned tunnel, all the while pointing the gun at her back.

As darkness descended, the doctor's car lights — which she had taken the precaution of leaving on — were noticed by local man Claude Jeremiah Greengrass, 55, going about his nocturnal business. He duly notified Ashfordly Police.

The doctor's husband, P.C. Nick Rowan, ventured into the tunnel and managed to take the man into custody without a struggle.

PATIENT

Londoner Frank Robinson, whose current address was given as a boarding-house in Aidensfield, was charged with abduction and firearms offences. He will appear in court next week.

In an exclusive interview, Dr. Rowan recounted her ordeal to the *Gazette*. 'I was on my way to visit a little girl, Amy Reddle, who was sick. Just outside Aidensfield I saw a man by the roadside. I knew him as a patient at my surgery and I thought he was having another asthma attack so I pulled over. That was when he suddenly produced the gun.

TRAINING

'I couldn't believe what was happening. It's the sort of thing you might expect in London, but not in Aidensfield.

'I tried to remember all the things which my husband had told me to do should I ever find myself in such a situation. So I kept calm and attempted to leave clues so that I could be found. That's why when we reached the sidings I deliberately left the car lights on. I was just hoping someone would see them and think there was something suspicious.'

(continued on page 6)

DOCTOR'S GUN TERROR

(continued from page 5)

'It was dark and smelly in the tunnel. I've never been so scared in my life. But I didn't want him to know that.

'I tried to strike up a dialogue with the man, to find out why he had kidnapped me. He said that my husband had arrested his granddaughter when he worked for the Metropolitan Police and had given evidence against her in court. Apparently the girl was found guilty of killing her lover who had been beating her up. Then when her grandmother died she became so depressed that she hanged herself in prison. It seemed that the man blamed Nick and had come to Aidensfield to avenge his granddaughter's death.

FAMILY AFFAIR — LIFE AND DEATH

'I could see that despite the gun he was a sensitive man and so I told him that the little girl I had been on my way to visit was desperately ill and needed a lifesaving injection. I could see he was moved by this and so I stood up to leave. He could have shot me at any second but somehow I sensed he wouldn't.

'Then suddenly he pointed the gun at himself, just as my husband arrived. I pleaded with the man not to do anything silly and eventually he handed me the gun. I was just so relieved when it was all over. And the first thing I did was make my visit to young Amy Reddle.'

More fun from Aidensfield fête.

GREENGRASS HELPS WITH ENQUIRIES

Sgt. Oscar Blaketon added: 'We are extremely grateful to Mr. Greengrass for his show of public spiritedness, although I understand that his tongue was loosened somewhat by the knowledge that we weren't going to prosecute him for poaching.'

MAN REMANDED

Chauffeur Michael Lewis of Ashfordly Hall was remanded in custody at Ashfordly Magistrates' Court this week on a charge of armed robbery. He is accused of robbing market trader Joe Duffy at Elsinby Moor on 29 January.

RELIABLE USED AUSTIN VANS
WIDE RANGE OF MODELS
1958 to 1965 – VARIOUS PRICES.
WORK SHOP TESTED
HARRISON'S GARAGE
UPGANG LANE & STATION SQ., WHITBY.
Tel. 1321/2/3.

Ashfordly Gazette

With which is incorporated the "Ashfordly Times and North Yorkshire Advertiser"

Registered at the General Post Office as a Newspaper. | Established 1856 No. 5691. | Printed and Published by HORNE & SON, LIMITED, WHITBY | FRIDAY, FEBRUARY 26th, 1965. | 12 Pages. | Price 3d. | Tel. 396 (Editorial Tel. 1070)

AIDENSFIELD EDITION

THREE WOMEN HELD AFTER ARMED ROBBERIES

Police Officer And Publican Locked In Cellar For Evening

Amiss Family Robinson: Mother Nell (centre) with Jean (left) and Susan.

Three local women — all from the same family — were arrested yesterday after two violent armed robberies in three days had terrorised the village of Aidensfield. The three — a mother and two daughters in their twenties — were taken to Ashfordly Police Station following a police swoop on a house on the outskirts of town.

ENFORCED LOCK-IN

The drama began on Sunday night. George Ward, landlord of the Aidensfield Arms, and one of his regular customers, Claude Jeremiah Greengrass, were held at gunpoint by three masked robbers an hour after closing time. When P.C. Nick Rowan saw lights on in the pub and went to investigate, he too was seized by a raider wearing a navy blue boiler suit and a dark balaclava with eye slits.

P.C. Rowan was then knocked out by a blow to the head and the three captives were bundled into the pub cellar where Mr. Greengrass was forced to handcuff the Constable. The robbers made off with the contents of the pub till, thought to be as much as £30. Their getaway van was seen heading off on the York road.

It was not until the following morning that the men were rescued by a drayman delivering beer to the Aidensfield Arms. P.C. Rowan was treated for his injuries by his wife, Dr. Kate Rowan.

'It was a frightening experience,' said Mr. Greengrass, 59. 'Even putting the Constable in handcuffs couldn't make up for the trauma I went through. And they made off with a brace of pheasants I'd come by — perfectly legitimately, of course.'

The second robbery took place at Aidensfield Post Office on Wednesday morning at around 11.30. A small amount of cash was taken. Again there were no descriptions of the culprits.

The police homed in on the suspects' house, at Vale Road, Ashfordly, following a tip-off.

One of the suspects is believed to have tried to resist arrest by pulling a gun on P.C. Rowan. The women were named by Ashfordly Police as Nell Robinson and her daughters Susan and Jean.

HUSBANDS AND WIVES

It is understood that Nell Robinson is the wife of the late Alec Robinson who had a string of convictions for armed robbery. Robinson is thought to have died of a heart attack during a recent robbery in Scarborough and to have been dumped on the doorstep of his house by his fellow criminals. According to the police, the family buried him in secret and concealed his death so that they could claim National Assistance.

Charges are expected to follow over the weekend.

THE WORLD ABOUT US

– Widespread protests followed British Rail's announcement to cut the rail network by half, based on the Beeching report.

– Black Muslim leader Malcolm X was shot dead in New York, not long after severing links with the Nation Of Islam.

– Stan Laurel, the slimmer partner of the famous Laurel and Hardy comedy duo, died.

– Distillers started a whisky price war by selling scotch at 7s 0d a bottle.

FARMER SHOT HIMSELF AFTER FOOT-AND-MOUTH OUTBREAK

— Couldn't Bear To Hear Cattle Frying

The Ashfordly Coroner found this week that local farmer Reg Manston had committed suicide, probably due to depression over a recent outbreak of foot-and-mouth disease at his farm.

Mr. Manston's body was discovered at a bleak spot on Kirlby Moor on 11 March after his son had reported him missing. His shotgun and faithful border collie were by his side.

SICK SHEEP

The outbreak had been reported to Aidensfield-based P.C. Nick Rowan two days previously by postmistress Edith Armstrong. Delivering letters on foot to Mr. Manston's remote Elmbeck Farm, she spotted a sick cow in a field. Veterinary examination revealed that the animal was foaming at the mouth, confirming foot-and-mouth disease.

Disinfectant dips and 'Keep Out' notices were placed at all farm entrances in the area and strict quarantine regulations were introduced.

When the vets and slaughtermen arrived to shoot Mr. Manston's pedigree herd, the distraught farmer, who had spent years building up his business, initially refused to let them enter. He stood at his gate guarding his farm with a shotgun and it needed the persuasive powers of P.C. Rowan to bring an end to the deadlock.

HEARTBREAKING DECISION

Eventually Mr. Manston realised that he had no option but to allow access but he was still visibly upset when the first shots rang out. He was unable to watch the huge funeral pyre which marked the burning of the infected carcasses. As the slaughtermen left, he wandered off up the moor for the last time.

Mr. Manston's next-door farmer, Sam Carver, faces prosecution arising from claims that he deliberately tried to evade road-blocks with a lorry full of infected sheep which he intended to offload at Ashfordly Market. His night-time mission was halted by Ashfordly Police who are expected to prefer charges this week.

Farmer Reg Manston had to be restrained while his herd was slaughtered. He shot himself while his sheepdog, faithful to the end, lay beside him.

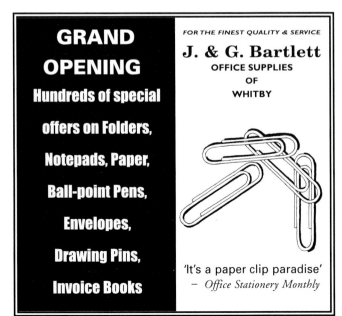

18-year-old Gina Ward takes the applause for winning Saturday's local talent contest.

THE LOCAL TALENT

Gina Ward, attractive 18-year-old niece of Aidensfield Arms landlord George Ward, won a talent contest at her uncle's pub on Saturday night. A lively singer with an ear for a tune, Miss Ward has recently moved to the area from Liverpool.

Publican George Ward came fifth as W. C. Fields.

BURGLARY CASE REVIEWED

Ashfordly Police revealed this week that they have forwarded new information to the Home Office which could lead to the release of a man jailed for burglary 18 months ago.

Terence Tinniswood of York Road, Aidensfield, is currently serving a four-year sentence for burglary in Strangeways Prison, Manchester, following a break-in at the Aidensfield home of Miss Irene Hamilton on 28 August 1963. Miss Hamilton disturbed the burglar who hit her over the head with a blunt instrument. York Assizes heard how a blood-stained pickaxe handle was later found in Tinniswood's van.

But new evidence suggests that Tinniswood — whom police nicknamed 'Teflon Terry' because they could never get anything to stick to him — may have been framed by an officer now retired from the force.

The arresting officer, P.C. Rowley Cussons, took early retirement shortly after the case, apparently because of ill-health. A police spokesman would not confirm that P.C. Cussons' successor, Nick Rowan, had been unable to find the case file when he began investigating claims that Tinniswood had been wrongly convicted.

Nor would anyone from Ashfordly Police comment on allegations that Cussons has admitted planting the pick-axe handle.

The case was highlighted after Tinniswood's wife Rosie took an overdose to draw attention to her husband's innocence. Yesterday she welcomed the fresh developments. 'I always knew my Terry had been stitched up,' she told the *Gazette*.

P.C. ATTACKED ON STAG NIGHT

P.C. Phil Bellamy of Ashfordly Police was left unconscious following a vicious attack on his stag night last Friday.

P.C. Bellamy had enjoyed a convivial evening in the Aidensfield Arms with colleagues. It was while he was hand-cuffed to a lamp-post outside the inn singing an impromptu version of 'Ticket To Ride' that he was struck over the head.

The next morning P.C. Bellamy recognised his assailant when he discovered him in bed with his bride-to-be. The wedding, scheduled for St. Michael's Church, Eltering, that afternoon, was called off.

RACEHORSE BANNED

Claude Jeremiah Greengrass, owner of the 'problem' racehorse, with his tasteful new car.

— Affluent Effluent

Police have banned a local racehorse from using the grass verge in the centre of Aidensfield as a gallop. The move follows complaints from residents.

One, who wished to remain unnamed, told the *Gazette*: 'I don't want to have to dodge in and out of clattering hooves every time I visit the village shop. Then there's the mess.

It might be good for my roses but it does nothing for the soles of my Hush Puppies.'

Police said the pile of manure at the junction of York Road and Moor Lane should be treated as a roundabout.

HORSE PLAY

The horse is owned by local man Claude Jeremiah Greengrass, 70, who recently came into a sizeable sum of money following the sale of a patch of waste land to the Ministry of Defence. Mr. Greengrass has also purchased a bright pink American Cadillac which has become a familiar sight in the village.

He said of the ban: 'It's victimisa ..., it's victi ... the police have got it in for me.'

CAR AND OWNER BOTH GUTTED IN ARSON

Claude Jeremiah Greengrass shouts angrily at reporters yesterday after his car was destroyed by fire.

Local businessman Claude Jeremiah Greengrass, 57, was inconsolable last night after his beloved pink Cadillac car was destroyed in a fire.

Two youths, Barry Phillips and Neil Hendon, were charged with starting the blaze at a lock-up garage on the outskirts of Aidensfield. They are also expected to be charged with a burglary at Dr. Ferrenby's surgery on Monday — during which the doctor was hit over the head — and with supplying drugs.

MORE CASUALTIES

Dr. Ferrenby was last night described as 'stable' by Ashfordly Cottage Hospital. Also detained in the hospital was Pickering teenager Deborah Wilson who collapsed in the Aidensfield Arms. Her illness is thought to be drug-related.

THE WORLD ABOUT US

– Former world light-heavyweight boxing champion Freddie Mills was found shot dead in a car in London's Soho.

– Edward Heath succeeded Sir Alec Douglas-Home as Conservative Party leader.

– The Beatles' film *Help!* premiered in London.

– Space-exploration vessel Mariner IV sent back photographs of the surface of Mars.

Ashfordly Gazette

With which is incorporated the "Ashfordly Times and North Yorkshire Advertiser"

Registered at the General
Post Office as a Newspaper | Established 1856 No. 5729. | Printed and Published by HORNE & SON. LIMITED. WHITBY | FRIDAY, NOVEMBER 19th, 1965. | 12 Pages. | Price 3d. | Tel. 396 (Editorial Tel. 1070)

AIDENSFIELD EDITION

HUNDREDS INVOLVED AS TRAIN DERAILED IN SNOW CHAOS

— Aidensfield Cut Off By Blizzard

P.C. Nick Rowan (right) with some of the evacuated passengers.

Gina Ward of the Aidensfield Arms tends to her injured brother, Barry.

The coldest November temperatures for 73 years brought misery to the North York Moors this week with a number of villages cut off by heavy falls of snow. At the height of the blizzard on Tuesday night, a train crashed on frozen points south of Aidensfield station.

The eight-carriage train — the 7.14 from Pickering — was carrying 180 passengers when it was derailed 200 yards from Aidensfield shortly before 8pm. Carriages were strewn across the track and dazed passengers struggled to climb free of the wreckage.

'BLOODY MESS' SAYS FIRST P.C. ON SCENE

One of the first people on the scene was, not surprisingly, a Police Constable from the local station, Nick Rowan. 'It was a right mess,' he said. 'There was a lot of blood and some passengers were clearly in a distressed state. I saw a little girl carrying a blood-splattered doll, crying for her mum. Fortunately her mother was OK — they'd simply become separated in all the confusion.

(continued on page 2)

TRAIN CRASH HORROR

P.C. Nick Rowan (right) with the injured G.P., Dr. Alex Ferrenby.

(continued from page 1)

'The priority was to get everyone away from the scene of the accident. Most were able to walk under their own steam but others needed help. As news of the crash spread through the village, something like 100 volunteers turned out to lend a hand. It was real community spirit.'

DOCTORS IN TROUBLE

The passengers were ferried by residents to Aidensfield Village Hall where they received makeshift medical attention. The situation was not helped by the absence of a local doctor from the local practice, Dr. Kate Rowan, who was at the time stranded on the moors with a heavily pregnant patient.

And among those injured in the rail crash was the village's other G.P., Dr. Alex Ferrenby, who sustained cuts and bruises to the head. Only four months ago, Dr. Ferrenby suffered head wounds during a robbery at his surgery. Most of the other injuries were superficial although one man was treated for a suspected broken leg.

LOCAL SAVIOUR

Despite power to Aidensfield being cut off for several hours, the village hall was rescued from darkness thanks to the efforts of local man Claude Jeremiah Greengrass, 56, who supplied a generator at reasonable rates.

Mr. Greengrass spent an anxious night worrying about the fate of his beloved lurcher Alfred, lost somewhere up on the moors. Happily the errant hound was eventually found by P.C. Rowan and returned to his grateful owner.

(continued on page 5)

SNOW HELL FOR VILLAGE

George Ward helps P.C. Nick Rowan at the height of the drama.

(continued from page 2)

Dr. Rowan also had to be rescued after driving up to isolated Rose Cottage to treat Mrs. Ellen Walsh who had gone into labour. When complications developed, Dr. Rowan decided to try and drive Mrs. Walsh down to Aidensfield but on the way her Land Rover skidded into a ditch.

LAST-DITCH RESCUE

With all roads in and out of Aidensfield blocked by snow, the two women faced the prospect of spending the night on the moors in freezing cold temperatures. But then Mrs. Walsh's former husband, Steven, turned up in a tractor and towed their vehicle back to the village hall. Shortly afterwards, Mrs. Walsh gave birth to a baby girl.

By Thursday lunchtime the situation had eased slightly and a snowplough had cleared the carriages from the track. Power had been restored to much of Aidensfield although most surrounding roads remained impassable.

FRIGHTENING PREDICTIONS

One man who was not caught out by the sudden cold snap was local amateur weather forecaster Raymond Snell. 'Although I didn't make it public at the time, I correctly predicted the bitter winter of 1962–63,' said Mr. Snell. 'And now I am convinced that this latest snowfall is an indication that we are heading back to the Ice Age.

'By the year 2000 the whole of Britain will be permanently frozen over and large polar bears will roam the arctic tundra that we once knew as Middlesbrough.'

Claude Jeremiah Greengrass.

GREYHOUND SWITCH FOILED

A plot to influence the result of the prestigious Maddleskirk Trophy race was foiled when the intended switching of dogs never took place.

Although details are still unclear, it appears that a plan was hatched to run a greyhound as what is termed a 'ringer' in Saturday's big race, the highlight of the season at Maddleskirk Stadium.

'FLASHY' SCAM FOILED

The mystery is thought to surround the greyhound Northern Flash, owned by property developer Jack Scarman. Northern Flash trailed in a disappointing fourth, in the process wrecking a huge gamble by his connections. However, a source told the *Gazette* that Northern Flash was meant to have been substituted just before the race by a quicker dog, trained by John Parrish. But, unbeknown to the backers of Northern Flash, the switch was foiled when Mr. Parrish found out what was going on.

After the race Mr. Scarman was seen in a heated exchange with local character Claude Jeremiah Greengrass, 66, who is also believed to have lost a considerable amount of money on Northern Flash.

GREENGRASS INVOLVEMENT

Neither of the men were prepared to comment on the allegations, but Aidensfield's Mr. Greengrass warned: 'If I find out who the allegator is, there'll be trouble.'

MATCH ABANDONED

— By 'Onlooker'

Saturday's eagerly-awaited clash between Aidensfield and Strensford was abandoned after only 15 minutes ... because of cows.

The herd had wandered on to the North Lane pitch before kick-off and despite the best efforts of all 22 players and the match officials, they refused to move.

Referee Mr. A. Harrow decided to start the game with the players trying to play around the cattle but this proved a futile exercise, not least because some of the animals were more mobile than the footballers.

Furthermore, the ball regularly landed in cow pats so that at one point there was a five-minute delay before anyone could be persuaded to take a throw-in.

Finally, when a goal-bound shot — well struck by the Strensford centre-forward — was headed off the Aidensfield goal-line by a Guernsey heifer with the custodian beaten, the referee realised that he had little alternative but to abandon proceedings.

VILLAGE MOURNS DEMISE OF LOCAL DOCTOR

Death In Fishing Accident

Dr. Alex Ferrenby, born and bred in Aidensfield, died this week on a fishing holiday in Wensleydale. He was 72.

Dr. Ferrenby, who has been the village G.P. for 41 years, drowned after falling in the River Ure near Askrigg. He had gone away to recuperate from injuries received in the Aidensfield train crash.

TALE OF TWO DOCTORS

His practice partner, Dr. Kate Rowan said: 'He was a caring, gentle man who will be greatly missed.' An inquest into his death is expected to be held before Christmas.

He'll be fondly remembered: Dr. Ferrenby of Aidensfield.

THE WORLD ABOUT US

– The government introduced an experimental 70 mph speed limit on motorways.

– Midlands housewife Mrs. Mary Whitehouse announced the setting-up of the National Viewers' and Listeners' Association to clean up television.

– Australian quartet The Seekers topped the hit parade with 'The Carnival Is Over'.

WEDDING DAY BLUES

Susan Siddons' wedding day at St. Michael's Church, Eltering, on Saturday turned into a chapter of disasters.

First, some of the wedding presents were stolen and then the church's floral displays, so lovingly arranged by Anne Whittaker of Ashfordly Flowers, were destroyed. Finally, the bride's father, Mr. Jack Siddons, was struck down by food poisoning shortly before the ceremony.

PRESENTS NOT PRESENT

The presents, including the latest model in transistor radios, were later found dumped in nearby bushes. Peter Begg, a jealous former boyfriend of the bride, subsequently admitted to P.C. Nick Rowan that he had been responsible both for stealing the presents and trashing the flowers.

'PRESENTS NOT POISON'

But Begg denied any responsibility for poisoning the father of the bride whose illness proved to be the result of having eaten poorly-stored prawns. The prawns, thought to have been part of a haul of stolen shellfish snatched from a lorry in Aidensfield, had been sold to Mr. Siddons by local businessman Claude Jeremiah Greengrass, 62.

Police are continuing with their inquiries.

MOTHER AND SON DECLARED GUILTY OF GRAVE-ROBBING

Removed Corpse's Trousers

At the end of a two-day trial at York Assizes, Aidensfield woman Betty Sutch and her son Simon were each sentenced to 18 months' imprisonment after being found guilty of grave-robbing, assaulting a police officer and passing forged banknotes.

The pair, who pleaded not guilty to all three charges, were convicted by the jury after just 20 minutes' deliberation.

NOTE FROM BEYOND THE GRAVE

The court heard how Mrs. Sutch had stumbled across a letter from her late husband Arthur telling her that the key to his safety deposit box was in the trouser pocket of his best suit. Realising that Mr. Sutch had been buried in his best suit, she and her son proceeded to rob the grave in order to get their hands on the key that they thought would bring them wealth.

P.C. Nick Rowan described how he was patrolling Aidensfield on the night of 13 September when he noticed a light in the churchyard. Investigating further, he found a partially-opened grave. Seconds later, he was hit over the head with a spade and knocked unconscious.

Seeing that the grave belonged to Arthur Sutch, P.C. Rowan visited the family

The mother-and-son team that caused so much trouble.

the following day at their piggery just outside the village. They denied any involvement in the affair.

REVENGE FROM BEYOND THE GRAVE

Two nights later, the Sutch grave was interfered with again. This time the coffin was opened and the corpse's trousers stolen.

The following week a number of forged banknotes turned up in the cashbox at the Aidensfield Arms. Pretty barmaid Gina Ward testified

that they had been used by Betty Sutch to buy a quantity of alcohol for a party. The forged notes were subsequently traced to Arthur Sutch's safety deposit box.

In summing up, Judge Milton Harrap said that Mrs. Sutch had clearly been set up by her late husband from whom she had been estranged during the last years of his life.

But, he added, any mitigating circumstances were nullified by the 'sheer greed' which she and her son had displayed.

POLICE SWOOP ON BADGER BAITERS

— Gang Held After Furious Struggle

Ashfordly Police arrested a seven-man gang of badger baiters on Wednesday following a carefully-planned operation.

The gang and their terriers had just arrived at a sett in Aidensfield Wood when police officers swooped from their hiding places behind trees and bushes. As the men tried to escape, a pitched battle broke out as a result of which two officers needed treatment for minor cuts.

MAJOR FRACAS

Six Middlesbrough men and one from Aidensfield — animal feed delivery man Harry Capshaw — have been charged with offences including assaulting police officers. They will appear at Ashfordly Magistrates' Court on Monday.

The covert police operation followed a circular from Division warning that a number of 'sportsmen' from Middlesbrough were targeting the Aidensfield area in search of animals to bait.

POLICE FOREWARNED

Last week a local man, David Stockwell, discovered a badger sett that had been dug out. A dead badger lay nearby but another animal, although wounded, was still alive and Mr. Stockwell took it to Dr. Kate Rowan for treatment.

(continued on page 4)

David Stockwell pictured with a rescued badger.

AIDENSFIELD G.P. INQUEST

The inquest on Aidensfield G.P. Alex Ferrenby, who drowned on a fishing holiday last month, revealed that he had been suffering from a slow brain haemorrhage. It is believed that the condition, which may have been caused by a blow to the head received during a burglary in July, made him feel disorientated and fall into the river.

The Coroner recorded an open verdict.

CORRECTION

It seems that the initials found carved on a pew in Aidensfield Church — SH 1T — and reported in last week's *Gazette* as being probably over 100 years old were not, in fact, those of Stephen Hunter of said class. After much careful checking by the *Gazette*'s staff, it looks as though there has never been such a class or name at the local school.

'Scum of the Earth' — the recently apprehended gang of badger baiters, according to Sgt. Oscar Blaketon.

WHAT'S ON

· · · · · · · · · · · · · · · · ·

Saturday. Whitby Essoldo. Dave Berry and the Cruisers. Doors Open 7.30pm. Admission 8s 0d.

Saturday–Friday. Whitby Gaumont. *The Knack*. 3.10pm, 7.30pm.

Saturday–Friday. Ashfordly Regal. *The Sound of Music*. 2.45pm, 7.15pm.

Monday. St Peter's Church Hall. Whitby Trawlermen's Association Talk: 'Pay Offers — Should We Take The Bait?'

Tuesday. Aidensfield Village Hall. Brass-Rubbing Demonstration. 7.30pm. Admission Free.

Wednesday. Aidensfield Village Hall. Ashfordly Townswomen's Guild Debate: Do The Beatles Deserve Their MBEs? 2pm. Coffee 7d.

PERSONAL COLUMNS

EAR PIERCING — WHILE YOU WAIT.
9 Marshall St., Ashfordly. Open 9am–5.30pm, except Sundays.

BEAUTIFUL WEDDING-DRESS
Only used for going to shops. Large engine. Room for four people. Baby Seat Included. Damaged rear light, slight rust under rims. One careful lady owner. £225.
Tel: **ASH 312**

SECOND-HAND FORD CORTINA
Tidy, and complete with radio, net underskirt, floral headband and lace veil. Kept in box on top of wardrobe for 40 years. £5 19s 11d.
Tel: **ASH 335**

Wanted: Ring-tailed lemur from PG Tips' 'Wild Animals' card series. Will swap three polar bears, two echidnas and a western pocket gopher.
Tel: **ASH 341**

BADGER BAITING

(continued from page 2)

When Mr. Stockwell was then approached by a man offering him 10s for each sett he pointed out, he went to the police with the information. Officers decided to set a trap — not for the badgers, but for the baiters.

POLICE REACTION

Sgt. Oscar Blaketon was delighted with the outcome. 'Badger baiters are the scum of the earth,' he said. 'When they do get caught, they invariably get off lightly, but the fact that we have additionally been able to charge these men with assaulting police officers should ensure that the magistrates take a tougher line. All in all, a couple of swollen lips for our young lads is a small price to pay.'

THE WORLD ABOUT US

– Broadcaster Richard Dimbleby died of cancer, aged 52.

– Goldie, London Zoo's wayward golden eagle, is back in captivity after escaping for the second time this year.

– America celebrated the first rendezvous in space, made by two Gemini spacecraft.

– Plans were announced to introduce random breath tests to monitor motorists for alcohol.

```
TUITION
Learn tping in 10
lesons
from professional typist
TEL: ASH 359
```

Ashfordly Gazette

With which is incorporated the "Ashfordly Times and North Yorkshire Advertiser"

Registered at the General Post Office as a Newspaper | Established 1856 No. 5738. | Printed and Published by HORNE & SON. LIMITED. WHITBY | FRIDAY, JANUARY 21st, 1966. | 12 Pages. | Price 3d. | Tel. 396 (Editorial Tel. 1070)

AIDENSFIELD EDITION

BEAST OF THE MOORS: RIDDLE SOLVED

Two of Aidensfield's finest, seen here taking a well-earned break.

The mystery of the 'Beast of the Moors' which has ravaged sheep in the area was finally solved this week. And far from being an escaped puma or leopard, as some had speculated, it turned out to be nothing more than a large dog.

The so-called beast had left over 20 sheep dead in a series of attacks over the past three weeks. But it is hoped that its reign of terror is now over following the arrest of two men on the outskirts of Aidensfield on Wednesday evening. Pursued by P.C. Nick Rowan, their van crashed into a ditch on the Elsinby road when the driver lost control of the vehicle.

DOG OWNERS DETAINED

In the back of the van, P.C. Rowan discovered several sheep which had just been stolen from nearby Moor Farm and a large, savage dog. Stephen Cameron and David Slade, both from Aidensfield, are due to appear at Ashfordly Magistrates' Court next week. The dog will not be attending.

The hunt for the so-called 'beast' began on New Year's Day when three ewes were found savaged near Strensford.

As the attacks continued, experts became divided as to whether they were the work of rustlers or an escaped big cat, possibly a distant relative of the elusive 'Surrey Puma'.

NIGHT IN THE COLD FOR P.C.s

Senior policemen favoured the second theory and officers from Ashfordly Police Station were ordered to spend a cold night on the moors in search of the creature. The operation drew a blank.

With tension mounting, farmers began taking pot-shots at anything with four legs that moved. A couple, out courting on the moor, were very lucky to escape without serious injury.

News of the arrest of two human suspects and one canine came as a particular (continued on page 2)

Greengrass (right) and Alfred.

BEAST RIDDLE
(continued from page 1)

relief to local smallholder Claude Jeremiah Greengrass, 56, whose own dog, Alfred, had been sentenced to be destroyed for the attacks.

Alfred, a lurcher cross, had been missing for nearly two weeks — a period of time which coincided with the attacks. He finally returned home covered in white paint. Three days later, after a raid on his farm at Kirlby Moor, Ted Ditchley shot Alfred as the dog ran across fields.

The evidence of Mr. Ditchley plus the suspicious paint resulted in Ashfordly Magistrates ordering the dog to be destroyed. However, before the order could be carried out, Mr. Greengrass managed to smuggle his pet from the Police Station. Now his actions would appear to be vindicated.

INNOCENT DOG

'I hope people round here can now see that Alfred is as innocent as I am,' said Mr. Greengrass yesterday.

But it was not all good news. As Mr. Greengrass proudly paraded Alfred for photographers outside the Aidensfield Arms, he was accosted by an irate lady berating him about the behaviour of his dog.

The woman claimed that Alfred had mated with her two pedigree bitches despite her efforts to prevent it by throwing a tin of paint over him. Mr. Greengrass was later heard to be demanding a stud fee for his pet.

Ashfordly Gazette

With which is incorporated the "Ashfordly Times and North Yorkshire Advertiser"

Registered at the General Post Office as a Newspaper. | Established 1856 No. 5741. | Printed and Published by HORNE & SON. LIMITED. WHITBY | FRIDAY, FEBRUARY 11th, 1966. | 12 Pages. | Price 3½d. | Tel. 396 (Editorial Tel. 1070)

AIDENSFIELD EDITION

Dr. Rowan of Aidensfield surgery, who originally diagnosed Mr Swaby's illness.

AIDENSFIELD MAN DIES IN RABIES ALERT

— *Boy Critical After Hospital Dash*

Local garage mechanic Jim Swaby died in Ashfordly Cottage Hospital yesterday morning as an outbreak of rabies threatened to sweep the area. Last night a second victim, a teenage boy, was critically ill in the same hospital.

The epidemic is believed to have been caused by a retriever dog imported into this country from Germany in violation of quarantine regulations. Yesterday lunchtime the dog was shot in Birley Woods shortly after biting its young master, 14-year-old Jamie Halstead.

SPEEDY DEMISE OF VICTIM

Medical experts now hope that the outbreak has been contained. The scare began yesterday morning when Mr. Swaby called in at Dr. Kate Rowan's Aidensfield surgery complaining of headaches. As the day wore on, his condition worsened. Around 6pm, P.C. Nick Rowan took a newly-delivered police car to Swaby's garage for minor bodywork repairs. While he was there, Mr. Swaby suffered a violent spasm and P.C. Rowan rushed him to Ashfordly Hospital. There Dr. Rowan pronounced suspected rabies, a diagnosis confirmed by Dr. James Radcliffe, her practice partner at Whitby.

Dr. Rowan and Dr. Radcliffe immediately set about ascertaining whether Mr. Swaby had been bitten or come into contact with any animals recently.

(continued on page 2)

RABIES DEATH

(continued from page 1)

Mr. Swaby was able to recall a left-hand drive Opel car coming into the garage. He remembered that the occupants owned a friendly dog and told him that they were camping in the area. He added that he had subsequently seen the driver in the Aidensfield Arms.

Twelve hours later, Mr. Swaby was dead.

EARLY POLICE INVOLVEMENT

Officers from Ashfordly searched all camp sites in the area for vehicles which matched the description. A likely car was found at Birley Moor campsite minus its owners. A vehicle registration check with the ferry companies showed that it was an Opel Record brought in from Germany by Major Michael Halstead.

Sgt. Oscar Blaketon of Ashfordly Police contacted the Ministry of Agriculture regarding the rabies outbreak. As a result, road blocks were set up around a 12-mile radius of Birley Moor in the hope of containing the disease.

EXTREME MEASURES FOR SITUATION

Instructions were also issued that no animal was to be brought into the infected area; no animal was to be removed from the infected area without a special licence; all dogs were to be muzzled; all cats were to be kept indoors; all strays were to be rounded up; and all feral cats were to be shot on sight. And all hunting in the area was temporarily suspended.

Dr. James Radcliffe, Dr. Rowan's practice partner at Whitby.

DESPERATE SEARCH FOR OWNERS

Meanwhile the search for the Halstead family stretched from Sheffield in the south to Newcastle in the north. As panic spread, groups of men wielding shotguns and garden forks began combing the Aidensfield area looking for any stray animals to kill. Local gamekeepers were also mobilised.

(continued on page 8)

RABIES DRAMA
(continued from page 2)

Major Halstead was soon traced much closer to home. Gina Ward, the fetching young barmaid at the Aidensfield Arms, told P.C. Rowan that a stranger had come in the previous day to report a missing dog. He had left his name on the notice-board by the bar. When he returned for news of the dog, P.C. Rowan was waiting for him.

MILITARY MAN CHARGED

Major Halstead was taken to Ashfordly Police Station and charged with breaching the Importation of Dogs and Cats Order, 1928. He could face a fine of as much as £300.

With reports of a beagle belonging to local breeder Tom Gordon and a fox being found dead in suspicious circumstances in the area of Birley Wood, Mrs. Halstead was stopped at a roadblock on the Strensford road. She told

police officers that her son Jamie had gone off towards Birley Wood to search for his missing pet retriever, Sam.

Police quickly closed in on the wood and found the boy moments after he had been bitten by his dog. Local citizen Claude Jeremiah Greengrass, 55, shot the dog dead as it was about to attack again.

The boy was rushed for an urgent innoculation but remains in a critical condition. Nevertheless doctors at Ashfordly Cottage Hospital are hopeful that he will pull through.

MAN WILL BE MISSED

Last night Aidensfield was still in shock over the death of Mr. Swaby. One regular in the Aidensfield Arms, who did not wish to be named, said: 'The bloke who owned the dog wants stringing up.'

An emergency number has been set up to deal with the rabies outbreak. It is Ashfordly 377.

P.C. Nick Rowan originally drove Mr. Swaby to Ashfordly Hospital.

THE WORLD ABOUT US

– Watneys announced that they are putting up the price of a pint of bitter to 1s 8d.

– Businessman Freddie Laker has set up an airline for cut-price holidays.

– CND supporters picketed a London theatre screening of *The War Game*, the BBC's controversial film about an H-bomb attack on Britain. The film has already been banned from television transmission by the Corporation.

DRIVERLESS POLICE CAR PLOUGHS INTO STONEWORK

Police Erect Wall Of Silence

A driverless police car last night ran backwards down an Aidensfield hill and crashed straight into a stone wall.

According to unconfirmed reports, the car — a newly-delivered police vehicle — had been driven to Aidensfield Police House by P.C. Alfred Ventress of Ashfordly Police. Before entering the house, P.C. Ventress is thought to have forgotten to put the handbrake on.

He emerged moments later to see the car rolling away from him down the hill and was powerless to prevent a collision with the wall.

COMMUNITY POLICING

It is also thought that the car was involved in an accident earlier in the day when it apparently reversed into a truck owned by local man Claude Jeremiah Greengrass, 64. Mr. Greengrass, who is a popular figure in Aidensfield, says he will be pressing for compensation.

Sgt. Oscar Blaketon refused to comment specifically on the incidents but did promise, 'The matter will be dealt with by me internally and those responsible will be dealt with accordingly … even if that means some of the men having to take elementary driving lessons.'

Before hitting the wall, the runaway police car also knocked over and crushed three boxes of imported strawberries and a large vat of sugar.

'We're in a jam,' admitted one officer who did not wish to be identified.

P.C. Ventress in thoughtful mood.

PLAYERS TRIUMPH

The production of Shaw's 'St. Joan' at Aidensfield Village Hall was another triumph for the Aidensfield Players.

The whole cast handled their parts with relish and although the Dauphin's broad Yorkshire dialect may have dismayed some purists, it was well received here.

And there was a truly dramatic ending when the flames surrounding the martyr got out of control and had to be extinguished by uniformed members of Ashfordly Fire Brigade rushing on stage with their hoses.

If only the famous French peasant girl had had the benefit of such facilities 500 years ago …

WHITBY P.C. GUILTY OF BARMAID ATTACKS

'Drive Of Terror' Followed Rugby Match, Said Local Girl Who Fled To Woods

Elizabeth Rogers: Little's second victim.

Whitby-based Police Constable Simon Little was sentenced to five years' imprisonment at York Assizes on Thursday after being found guilty of two terrifying assaults on barmaids.

Among his victims was Gina Ward of the Aidensfield Arms who told the court that she feared for her life when Little pounced on her in the woods at night.

Wearing a clinging white top, dainty pink miniskirt and slender white knee-length boots, Miss Ward told the story of the evening's events; how she had attended a rugby match between North Riding Police and the Harbourmen in Whitby on 8 January.

After the match, in which Little had played, she had joined in the celebrations — with many others — at the town's Mermaid Inn.

DON'T DRINK AND DRIVE

'Dr. Rowan and his wife offered me a lift back to Aidensfield but I said no because I'd brought my own car. It was a good night but I wasn't drunk or anything, not with having to drive.

'I eventually left around closing time and set off for home. But about two miles from Aidensfield I became aware that a car was following me. It was a really dark, lonely stretch of road with no houses or lights.

SAFETY IN THE WOODS?

'The car seemed to be getting closer and closer. I started to panic. When I reached a junction, I stalled the car. I tried to restart it, but it wouldn't go. I was just so scared. Then in my mirror I could see this figure getting out of the car behind. I was terrified, just thinking that he was going to attack me so I made a run for it — into some woods.

(continued on page 6)

A Gazette photographer captures Miss Rogers being followed home by Little.

BARMAID ASSAULTS

(continued from page 5)

'I just prayed that I could get away from him but he caught me up and jumped on me. Luckily something — which I later found out was a piglet — squealed on being caught by Mr. Greengrass, who happened to be out in the woods as well that night, and that frightened my attacker off. I'm sure he would have killed me otherwise. I then ran home as fast as I could.'

DIFFICULT INVESTIGATION

At first police officers had little to act on but the discovery in Miss Ward's car of a tie belonging to P.C. Phil Bellamy of Ashfordly Police threw new light on the investigation. P.C. Bellamy insisted that Miss Ward had asked him to sit in the car on the night in question because she had been pestered at the Mermaid Inn by P.C. Neil Gibson from the Whitby force. P.C. Gibson vehemently denied the accusation or the speculation that he was involved in the subsequent attack on her.

After receiving threats from the Gibson family and convinced that the police did not believe her, Miss Ward took it upon herself to withdraw her statement about the assault.

But Police Constable Nick Rowan still harboured suspicions and so decided to return to the Mermaid Inn on the night of Saturday 15 January. Whilst there, he was told that the barmaid, Elizabeth Rogers, had gone home early because she thought that someone had been following her.

ROWAN GETS HIS MAN

Setting off in pursuit, P.C. Rowan spotted a man following Miss Rogers and gave chase. Initially, the man escaped through the dark streets and P.C. Rowan saw Miss Rogers home — safely, as he saw it — to her flat in North Street. No sooner had he turned to leave than the officer heard screams coming from inside the flat.

Miss Rogers' assailant had been lying in wait. Dashing to the rescue, P.C. Rowan arrested Little.

LITTLE BELITTLED

Miss Ward later picked out Little as her attacker at an identity parade.

After Little was sentenced Miss Ward told the *Gazette*: 'I'm just so relieved it's all over. And I'm so grateful to P.C. Rowan for believing my story from the start.'

THE WORLD ABOUT US

- The Football World Cup — owned by FIFA — has been stolen from Westminster Central Hall.

- Arkle received a hero's welcome in Ireland after winning the Cheltenham Gold Cup for the third time.

- In Rome the Pope and the Archbishop of Canterbury conducted the first official meeting for 400 years between the heads of the Roman Catholic and Anglican churches.

AMNESIA MAN CLEARED OF WAGES SNATCH

Seven-Year Bank Robbery Mystery Solved At Last

An Aidensfield man who left behind his family and his memory seven years ago has been cleared of a wages snatch after Ashfordly Police uncovered some new evidence.

Wages clerk Dennis Parker had been wanted for questioning for many years, in connection with the disappearance of £900 in May 1959. He vanished from Aidensfield on the very same day the money went missing, leaving behind his wife Helen and daughter Joanna, and had not been heard of since. Neither he nor the money had ever been traced.

RETURN OF THE NATIVE

But last Friday he dramatically turned up again in Aidensfield, saying he was looking for his family. He claimed to have no recollection of the last seven years. The only thing he managed to remember was collecting the money from the bank — part of his job — and a mystery car.

Aidensfield-based P.C. Nick Rowan began looking into the theory that Mr. Parker may have been the victim of the wages snatch rather than the perpetrator. He subsequently found out that a car had been reported stolen in that area, on the day the money went missing.

Then Rutland Police revealed that seven years ago two men were stopped in the stolen car with £900 about their persons.

In charge of the case: Sgt. Blaketon of Ashfordly Police Station.

A GIRL IN TWO PORTS, BUT NOT BIGAMY

The final piece of the jigsaw fell into place following the discovery of the name tag 'John Selby' on Mr. Parker's jacket. Hampshire Police informed P.C. Rowan that Mr. Parker had another wife, Jean Selby. Mrs. Selby came forward to explain how she had found Mr. Parker wandering around near Oakham in need of hospital treatment a few hours after he had disappeared from Aidensfield.

(continued on page 9)

FLAMING CHEEK!

Aidensfield Fire Fighters can only look on as the blaze burns out of control.

An Aidensfield man was furious this week after his insurance company refused to pay out on a barn destroyed by fire.

Claude Jeremiah Greengrass, 63, saw his barn razed to the ground in the early hours of Sunday morning. But his hopes for compensation were dashed when his insurance company ruled that he was not covered because the building was being used for business purposes.

FAIR EXCHANGE?

'It's a gross injustice,' stormed Mr. Greengrass. 'I was approached by some bloke and asked whether I'd set fire to his workshop in return for him burning down my barn — for the insurance. Naturally I wanted nothing to do with something that was against the law but the bloke went and burned down my barn anyway. 'When I refused to touch his workshop, he went and kidnapped my dog. The coppers arrested him for arson but then, blow me, his place burnt down accidentally. And the insurance company are going to pay up! But I won't get a penny. I've got no barn and no money. It's a disgrace. I'm writing to my MP.'

A local man was last night helping police with their inquiries.

AMNESIA VICTIM
(Continued from page 8)

Acting on this new information, the police have decided to drop all charges against Mr. Parker.

He was last night believed to be attempting a reconciliation with his first family who are now living in Middlesbrough. As for his other 'wife', it emerged that he and Mrs. Selby weren't married at all even though they had been living together for the past seven years. Sadly for her, he has no recollection of her existence. Readers should all take note; such are the perils of living in sin.

P.C. Nick Rowan and Claude Jeremiah Greengrass inspect the damage.

THE WORLD ABOUT US

– The BBC launched a new situation comedy series, *Till Death Us Do Part*.

– Former actor Ronald Reagan won the Republican nomination for Governor of California.

– An unmanned U.S. Surveyor spaceship has landed on the moon.

Ashfordly Gazette

With which is incorporated the "Ashfordly Times and North Yorkshire Advertiser"

Registered at the General Post Office as a Newspaper   Established 1856 No. 5,758S.   Printed and Published by HORNE & SON, LIMITED, WHITBY   FRIDAY, JUNE 17th, 1966.   12 Pages.   Price 3½d.   Tel. 396 (Editorial Tel. 1070)

AIDENSFIELD EDITION

WORLD CUP SPECIAL EDITION

Next month England stages the biggest sporting event in its history — the finals of the World Cup. Local interest is high — not only with regard to the progress of the host nation but also because one set of group matches is being played here in the north-east. In this special four-page pull-out, we look forward to the tournament and ask the question that is on every football fan's lips: who will win the World Cup?

AIDENSFIELD PREPARES FOR KOREAN INVASION

Aidensfield this week welcomed the North Korean football team to its bosom with the prospect of as many as 100 supporters expected to arrive in the area over the next three weeks, writes Onlooker.

The North Koreans have chosen Aidensfield as their base while they compete in the World Cup at Ayresome Park, Middlesbrough. The little-known Koreans, making their first appearance in the World Cup finals, are in group four of the tournament, along with the USSR, Italy and Chile.

The 31-strong party — made up of 20 players and 11 officials — checked in to Ashfordly Grange Hotel on Wednesday evening following an eight-hour coach drive from London's Heathrow Airport.

The North Korean players unwind by watching television in one of the private rooms at Ashfordly Grange Hotel.

SHORT STAY?

Hotel manager Mr. Eric Dawkins said: 'We are honoured to have been chosen by the North Koreans for their stay in North Yorkshire and will do everything we can to make their time here as pleasurable as possible. They will be assured of our usual high standard of service.

'We do not know precisely how long they will be staying but they have only booked accommodation for the group matches. I understand that they are not terribly confident about reaching the quarter-finals.'

Speaking through an interpreter, a high-ranking official with the North Korean national team told the *Gazette*: 'We chose Aidensfield because it is only an hour by road from Middlesbrough. It is also in nice countryside which will lift the spirits of our players. It will be good for their morals.

'The people in Aidensfield seem to be very friendly. We did not want to stay in Middlesbrough itself because we feared that the players would be distracted by the bright lights. But I believe it is a beautiful city on a river. Someone told me it was not altogether unlike Paris. Maybe one day footballers from countries like Italy or Brazil will come to play for one of the teams in Middlesbrough. I am sure they would love the place and never want to go home.'

The North Korean players are expected to be joined soon by a happy band of supporters who will have journeyed half-way across the world to support their team. This competition is certainly stirring the imagination of the footballing public judging by the story about the Swiss fan who is planning to push a pram across Europe in order to see the finals.

(continued on page 2)

The entire North Korean team was caught on camera at Ayresome Park. They were practising goal celebrations: let's hope they get the chance to do it for real!

Already the folk of Aidensfield are laying out the red carpet for their guests. Local resident Claude Jeremiah Greengrass, 72, revealed: 'I shall be opening the rooms of my establishment to our Korean visitors at reasonable rates. I've got a spare mattress, two sleeping bags and an old armchair. And to make them feel at home I shall be laying on special authentic menus, depending on what I can get from the Golden Dragon in Whitby. 'After all, I don't want to see them taking a fancy to Alfred.'

Over at the Aidensfield Arms, landlord George Ward has three rooms to let. He is also planning to erect a television set in the public bar so that his regular customers can watch the matches. 'I don't like televisions in public houses,' admitted Mr. Ward, 'but you have to move with the times and give the public what they want.'

AYRESOME MATCHES

The North Koreans have three weeks in which to acclimatise before they play their first match against the USSR on 12 July. The following day they meet Chile and their last group match is against Italy on 19 July. All three matches are at Ayresome Park. The remaining group matches will take place at Roker Park, Sunderland.

Little is known about the North Koreans although their star players are believed to be inside-right Pak Doo Ik and outside-left Pak Seung Zin. Both showed up well at the team's first training session yesterday afternoon on the pitch of Aidensfield FC, watched by an enthusiastic crowd of 18, composed almost entirely of members of the 5th Aidensfield Brownie pack.

The Koreans qualified from the huge Africa, Asia and Australia zone but the opposition was significantly reduced by the withdrawal of all 16 African countries in protest over FIFA's allocation of only one finals place from the zone. In addition, South Africa were expelled for rule violation. The outcome was to be decided by a tournament in Cambodia but South Korea elected to boycott this because they preferred to concentrate on raising a team for the 1968 Olympic Games. This left just North Korea and Australia to contest a place in the finals. North Korea won the two-legged affair emphatically 6–1 and 3–1.

SIZE MATTERS

But the little Koreans face stiff competition in their group from the burly Russians who qualified at the expense of Wales, Greece and Denmark despite losing 2–1 to the Welsh in Cardiff.

Italy — World Cup winners in 1934 and 1938 — are the other favourites to go through to the last eight. They qualified at the expense of Scotland, Poland and Finland and are expected to do well. Their manager, Edmondo Fabbri, is sure of a hostile reception if they fail. Italian fans are fond of pelting vanquished heroes with over-ripe fruit.

Chile cannot be discounted either. A rugged outfit, they finished third in the 1962 finals which were staged in their own country. They qualified this time by beating Ecuador in a play-off.

So it's a tough prospect for North Korea. But they can be sure of one thing — the people of Aidensfield will be behind them all the way.

'ENGLAND ARE NO-HOPERS'

— England have no chance of winning the World Cup, writes Onlooker

Ramsey's Hopefuls: The full 27-man England squad, pictured here at Lilleshall, Shrops. Five of the players will not stay for the World Cup Finals.

It gives me no pleasure to type these words but it is a realistic appraisal of the facts. Whilst it is true that host nations traditionally have an excellent record in the event, I simply cannot share the confidence of manager Alf Ramsey who has already gone on record as saying that England will win the tournament.

With the honourable exception of Bobby Charlton, England's players are little more than honest toilers. They might be able to run all day but they do not possess the skill of sides such as Brazil, rightly installed as 7–2 favourites.

Those who fancy England to spring an upset point to the team's impressive record under Mr. Ramsey. Of the 34 games played since he took charge in February 1963, England have won 20, drawn eight and lost six. They beat Northern Ireland 8–3 in November 1963 and six months later put ten goals past the United States.

But it is one thing scoring a hatful of goals against poor opposition, another to compete with the best. Don't forget that immediately after the United States game, England crashed 5–1 to Brazil in the Little World Cup. And as recently as last October we lost at home to Austria who have not even qualified for the World Cup Finals.

TEAM TROUBLE

England's main problem is their wingers. The wide men such as Terry Paine, Peter Thompson and John Connelly have consistently failed to deliver the goods. Unless Mr. Ramsey does the unthinkable and dispenses with wingers altogether, I cannot see many goal-scoring chances coming the way of Jimmy Greaves.

The other thing which concerns me is Mr. Ramsey's blatant southern bias. He played for southern clubs and man-

aged a southern club before taking the England job. Why has he picked four men — Moore, Hurst, Peters and Byrne — from a moderate club like West Ham? Surely there are better players here in the north.

England have one last chance to get it right when they embark on a four-match tour next week, taking in games against Finland, Norway, Denmark and Poland. Then it is down to real business on July 11th with the opening World Cup game against Uruguay.

RAMSEY'S BOAST

This week Mr. Ramsey has kept his cards close to his chest at England's training centre at Lilleshall, Shropshire. He is shortly expected to announce the trimming of the 27-man squad down to a final 22.

The current 27 are: Gordon Banks (Leicester City), Ron

Springett (Sheffield Wednesday), Peter Bonetti (Chelsea), Jimmy Armfield (Blackpool), George Cohen (Fulham), Ray Wilson (Everton), Keith Newton (Blackburn Rovers), Gerry Byrne (Liverpool), Norbert Stiles (Manchester United), Gordon Milne (Liverpool), Jack Charlton (Leeds United), Ron Flowers (Wolverhampton Wanderers), Bobby Moore (West Ham United), Norman Hunter (Leeds United), Terry Paine (Southampton), Ian Callaghan (Liverpool), Alan Ball (Blackpool), Roger Hunt (Liverpool), Jimmy Greaves (Tottenham Hotspur), Johnny Byrne (West Ham United), Geoff Hurst (West Ham United), Martin Peters (West Ham United), Bobby Charlton (Manchester United), George Eastham (Arsenal), John Connelly (Manchester United), Peter Thompson (Liverpool) and Bobby Tambling (Chelsea).

WHO WILL WIN THE WORLD CUP?

We took to the streets of Aidensfield to ask local people who they thought would win the World Cup:

One of Mr. Greengrass' assistants furthering England's World Cup cause.

P.C. Nick Rowan: 'It's got to be Brazil. They play such fantastic football. And they've got Pele — the best player in the world.'

Dr. Kate Rowan: 'I don't know much about football, but I'll go for Brazil too. Didn't they win it last time?'

Gina Ward, barmaid at the Aidensfield Arms: 'England, definitely — if only because Bobby Moore has got lovely legs and a great smile.'

George Ward, landlord: 'It's England for me. We're as good as anyone on our day. And we're on home soil. If the crowd get behind our boys, I think we've got a great chance, especially if Jimmy Greaves gets among the goals.'

Major Reginald Vickers (Retired): 'I don't think the Germans will be far away — at least not far enough away for my liking. I have also heard encouraging things about Argentina. I am led to believe that they play a good clean game.'

P.C. Phil Bellamy: 'I like the sound of the Italians. Anyway they have the prettiest supporters.'

P.C. Alf Ventress: 'I don't think I'll be watching — all that running around is not for me.'

WORLD CUP BONANZA FOR VILLAGE

As World Cup fever gripped Aidensfield with the arrival of the North Korean team, villagers have already begun cashing in on their good fortune. 'It's the best thing that has happened in ages,' said Mr. Henshaw of Henshaw's Bakery. 'We've already sold over 50 commemorative cakes in the shape of a football boot. They're selling like ... hot cakes.'

Gina Ward, delectable barmaid at the Aidensfield Arms, agrees: 'The World Cup has really put Aidensfield on the map. Who knows, we might even have TV cameras filming here? Wouldn't that be exciting? And Uncle George is selling a special World Cup bitter called Nobby Stiles — it's got plenty of bite and quite a kick.'

REAL DEAL

Local entrepreneur Claude Jeremiah Greengrass, 66, has a wide range of World Cup merchandise for sale. 'It's all legit, nothing dodgy,' he says. 'I've got scarves, rattles, even toilet rolls in England white.

And I've got a genuine ball signed by the England squad — Stanley Matthews, Tom Finney, the lot.'

However Ashfordly Police revealed that at least one person did not appreciate all of Mr. Greengrass' wares. Sgt. Oscar Blaketon told the *Gazette*: 'An elderly lady called in to say that Greengrass had threatened to expose himself to her. But when we looked into the matter further it transpired that he had merely offered to show her his World Cup Willie.'

BRAVE DOCTOR IN CHURCH ROOF RESCUE

Doctor risks all to save wayward soldier's life — community expects end of lead-stealing

Aidensfield G.P. Dr. Kate Rowan bravely climbed 30ft. on to a church roof on Wednesday afternoon to tend to an injured man. The man, named as Private Michael Foster from Wetherby, is thought to have fallen from the tower of St. Luke's Church, Strensford, while in the act of stealing lead.

The alarm was raised by two elderly women who spotted the man lying on the roof. Dr. Rowan was summoned and, aided by local chimney sweep Eddie Vickers, she clambered up onto the church roof to check out the young soldier's possible injuries.

WOULDN'T FOLLOW P.C. HUBBY'S ADVICE

After being administered on-the-spot treatment, the man was taken off to Ashfordly Cottage Hospital for further treatment to his back and leg injuries.

Yesterday Dr. Rowan played down her heroism. 'My husband wasn't keen on me going up there, particularly as I am pregnant. But I explained to him that it was part of my job,

Private Michael Foster is carried away to the hospital by firemen as P.C. Nick Rowan looks on.

just as confronting dangerous criminals is part of his.'

The rescue followed the third reported lead theft in the past week. Only last Sunday a quantity of lead pipes were stolen from a farm near Elsinby and the following day a sizeable amount of lead was stripped from the roof of Aidensfield Church.

PLOT THICKENS — POLICE ALERT

A truck was seen driving away at speed from St. Luke's Church a few minutes before Private Foster's body was discovered. 'We think he must have had at least one accomplice,' said P.C. Alfred Ventress of Ashfordly Police. 'We shall continue to question him in hospital.'

Ashfordly Gazette

With which is incorporated the "Ashfordly Times and North Yorkshire Advertiser"

Registered at the General Post Office as a Newspaper   Established 1856 No. 5762.   Printed and Published by HORNE & SON. LIMITED. WHITBY   FRIDAY, JULY 15th, 1966.   12 Pages.   Price 3/-d.   Tel. 396 (Editorial Tel. 1070)

AIDENSFIELD EDITION

MAN CONFESSES TO 'TRACTOR MURDER'

— Farmer's Death 'Made To Look Like Accident' By Embittered Son

Village Bobby P.C. Nick Rowan (right) with his wife, Dr. Kate Rowan.

A man appeared pleading guilty at York Assizes on Thursday to the murder of his father in April. Darcy Jacob, whose address was given as Whitelands Farm Cottage, Aidensfield, admitted killing 77-year-old Samuel Jacob and disguising the death to make it look like a tractor accident. The judge is expected to pass sentence today (Friday).

The court heard that after killing his father, Darcy persuaded his younger brother Arthur to cover up the crime. But the pair fell out when Samuel Jacob's will left his farm to Arthur instead. As the older brother, Darcy had expected to inherit.

ROBBERY AND VANDALISM

Darcy continued to live in the farm cottage but grew ever more resentful. Two weeks ago Arthur and his wife Emily returned home from holiday to find that their farmhouse home had been burgled and their cattle had been set free.

P.C. Nick Rowan, the officer called to the scene, described how the house had been ransacked. 'The place was in a real mess but the funny thing was the only items reported stolen were some silver and a record player. The other odd thing was that in spite of all the noise the burglar must have made, Darcy Jacob, who lived in a cottage on the farm, claimed he heard nothing.'

EVERY RECORD TELLS A STORY

A few days later, the stolen record player turned up at the Aidensfield Arms where it had been given to pert barmaid Gina Ward by a friend, Billy Redshaw. Questioned by the police, Mr. Redshaw said he had bought the gramophone player from local wheeler and dealer, Claude Jeremiah Greengrass, 69.

(continued on page 3)

Arresting officer Sgt. Oscar Blaketon.

TRACTOR MURDER
(continued from page 1)

Mr. Greengrass in turn told the police that the record player and a canteen of cutlery had been sold to him by Darcy Jacob.

While officers searched for Darcy, he turned up on the doorstep of the Police House in Aidensfield where Emily Jacob was staying. The court heard how she was petrified of Darcy and had sought refuge with Dr. Kate Rowan. Becoming increasingly unstable, Darcy broke into the Police House and abducted Mrs. Jacob. But before he could make his escape, he was arrested by P.C. Rowan and Sgt. Oscar Blaketon.

Asked about the burglary, Darcy confessed saying that he had needed to raise money in order to contest the will. But his biggest secret was revealed when Arthur, appalled by Darcy's bullying tactics, told the police that his father had met a violent death at Darcy's hand. Darcy broke down and confirmed the story. Charges against him of abduction were dropped. No charges were pressed against Arthur Jacob.

Ashfordly Gazette

With which is incorporated the "Ashfordly Times and North Yorkshire Advertiser"

Registered at the General Post Office as a Newspaper — Established 1856 No. 5763. — Printed and Published by HORNE & SON, LIMITED, WHITBY — FRIDAY, JULY 22nd, 1966. — 12 Pages. — Price 3½d. — Tel. 396 (Editorial Tel. 1070)

AIDENSFIELD EDITION

SHOTGUN DEATH OF CHICKEN FARMER

Local entrepreneur Claude Jeremiah Greengrass promoting his latest enterprise.

— Fowl Play Suspected

The discovery of the body of an Aidensfield chicken farmer has sparked a full-scale murder inquiry this week.

Mervyn Sykes was found shot dead on Thursday morning at Rongar Farm on the Elsinby road. It is thought that he had been killed by a shotgun some time during the previous night.

His blood-spattered body was discovered by one of his employees, Ken Appleby. Nearby police found a spent flashbulb, thought most likely to have come from a hand-held camera.

'There is no obvious motive at the moment,' commented Sgt. Oscar Blaketon of Ashfordly Police. 'And until we get the post-mortem, we can't even be sure that Mr. Sykes was murdered. So we are keeping an open mind. However, we have to consider the possibility that his death was suspicious, particularly in view of a number of other attacks on battery farms in Yorkshire and the fact that Mr. Sykes had been targeted personally.

APPEALING POLICEMEN

'We know that he had received poison pen letters and only last week his farm was daubed with crude writing — graffiti, I believe they call it. We also have reason to believe that he recently had an altercation with a photographer and we appeal for that person to come forward so that we can eliminate him from our inquiries.'

TRACTOR KILLER— LIFE IN PRISON

Darcy Jacob of Aidensfield, who confessed to the so-called 'tractor murder' of his father Samuel in April, was sentenced to life imprisonment at York Assizes last Friday.

Jacob — enlisting the help of his brother — had originally attempted to cover up the killing to make it look like an accident.

Ashfordly Gazette

With which is incorporated the "Ashfordly Times and North Yorkshire Advertiser"

Registered at the General Post Office as a Newspaper — Established 1856 No. 5764. — Printed and Published by HORNE & SON, LIMITED, WHITBY — FRIDAY, JULY 29th, 1966. — 12 Pages. — Price 3½d. — Tel. 396 (Editorial Tel. 1070)

AIDENSFIELD EDITION

BATTERY FARMER'S DEATH WAS AN ACCIDENT

Gun Went Off In Fracas With Photographer

Wife Responsible For Malicious Letters And 'Graffiti'—

P.C. Nick Rowan.

Ashfordly Police announced this week that the death of battery hen farmer Mervyn Sykes — found shot at Rongar Farm, Aidensfield, last Thursday — was no longer being treated as suspicious.

After the post-mortem into Mr. Sykes's death had proved inconclusive, police questioned an unnamed female photographer following the discovery of a spent flashbulb on the ground near the body.

She admitted going to Rongar Farm on the night of Wednesday 20 July but insisted that Mr. Sykes perished when his own shotgun went off. The police have accepted her version of events.

TIPPED-OFF

The hunt for the mystery photographer was stepped up after freelance lensman Edward Norton turned up at the murder scene on Friday morning. Questioned by police about the flashbulb, he said he had been given an anonymous tip-off by a woman.

Meanwhile P.C. Phil Bellamy had stumbled across a young woman countryside campaigner who was apparently staying at the Aidensfield Arms. On the morning after Mr. Sykes' death, P.C. Bellamy spotted the woman, her face cut and bruised, pushing her scooter towards Ashfordly.

(continued on page 6)

APOLOGY

The editor wishes to apologise to the family of the late Mr. Mervyn Sykes for the headline about his death on the front page of last week's *Gazette*. It was not our intention to be flippant and we deeply regret any distress which may have been caused.

FARM DEATH
(continued from page 1)

Later P.C. Bellamy asked P.C. Rowan to assist in the retrieval of the woman's scooter. P.C. Rowan discovered an empty camera case in a container on the scooter.

VITAL CLUES

Searching the surrounding countryside for the missing camera, the officers spotted marks on the road where the scooter had clearly skidded. On the grass verge they saw the camera. The flashbulb found at Rongar Farm fitted the camera perfectly.

P.C. Rowan also unearthed a bloodstained boiler suit — hidden in undergrowth on the road leading from Rongar Farm to Aidensfield village. It was subsequently sent for forensic testing.

The woman photographer was questioned about the death of Mervyn Sykes. P.C. Rowan told the *Gazette*: 'She admitted going to the farm that night to take photographs of the battery cages. She had already been chatted up by Mr. Sykes at the Aidensfield Arms and, because she did not want to be recognised, she wore a mask and boiler suit for her night-time mission.

'She said that as she started taking flash photographs of the cages, a dog began barking. This alerted Mr. Sykes who emerged brandishing a shotgun. He chased her until he cornered her and then hit her over the head with his shotgun. As he did so, the gun went off and he fell to the ground.

PROSECUTION PENDING

'All the evidence we have supports her story. But although she won't be charged with murder, she may well be prosecuted for breaking and entering or illegal trespass.

'The one thing she did deny,' added P.C. Rowan, 'was being responsible for painting the graffiti at Rongar Farm or sending the poison pen letters to Mr. Sykes. Those both turned out to be the work of Mr. Sykes' wife Monica.

SURPRISING REVELATION

'Mrs. Sykes not only despised her husband's womanising but also the whole concept of battery farming. It was she who had financed the business and she was angry at the direction it had taken. So she thought that by writing a few nasty letters and daubing slogans around the farm, she could worry him enough to get him to stop battery farming and return to more traditional farming methods. She'll never know whether her campaign would have worked.'

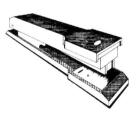

DRUNKEN DOG DISGRACE AT AIDENSFIELD FÊTE

— Lurcher Lives Up To Its Name

Claude Jeremiah Greengrass, owner of the hapless hound.

The Lurcher Challenge Cup competition at Saturday's Aidensfield Summer Fête was cancelled in controversial circumstances after one of the leading contenders was found drunk in the beer tent!

Alfred, owned by local character Claude Jeremiah Greengrass, 71, had been left unattended in the tent while Mr. Greengrass finalised the entry details. By the time he returned, the dog had consumed a quantity of beer slops and was considerably the worse for wear. He was scarcely able to put one paw in front of the other. With the other leading fancy, entered by Mr. Jeremiah Minto, falling victim to food poisoning, judges had little alternative but to abandon the contest.

ACCUSATION

Afterwards an angry Mr. Minto accused Mr. Greengrass of nobbling his animal by feeding him a doctored hot dog. 'That's rubbish is that,' countered Mr. Greengrass. 'He just wasn't such a hot dog after all.'

The fête — brought forward a week to avoid clashing with the World Cup final (a shrewd move in view of England's presence) — drew large crowds in warm sunshine. Ice cream vendors did a roaring trade and there was a novelty on the soft drinks stall with the introduction of cans with ring-pull ends. The Prize drinks — made in Lancashire — are believed to be the first to incorporate this new opening device which we at the *Gazette* are sure will catch on.

MINOR GUN TROUBLE

Apart from a minor fracas at the Guess the Weight of the Cake stall, the only other incident involved the theft of five firearms from the gun tent prior to the clay pigeon shooting competition. Thanks to the prompt actions of P.C. Nick Rowan, the weapons were quickly recovered from a hot dog van on the site. Two men will appear before Ashfordly Magistrates on Monday.

PROBATION AND FINE FOR FARMER GUILTY OF MALICIOUS DAMAGE

— *Child And Sheep*
Dragged Into Row

Dr. Kate Rowan: diagnosed brucellosis.

Kirlby Moor farmer Joseph Pitts was found guilty at Ashfordly Magistrates' Court on Wednesday of causing malicious damage towards neighbouring farmer Thomas Abbott. He was fined £250 and put on probation for a year.

The court heard how, over a period of several months, Pitts had tried unsuccessfully to buy the adjoining property of Mr. Abbott, a retired preacher. In a desperate bid to make Mr. Abbott change his mind, Pitts set about infecting the milk on his neighbour's farm and causing his sheep to escape.

INNOCENT INFANT

The sabotaged milk led 10-year-old Jane Shields to be struck down with brucellosis after she had been given a glass of unpasteurised milk by Mr. Abbott. On 11 August P.C. Nick Rowan investigated a complaint by Pitts that Mr. Abbott's sheep had strayed onto his land. On the same day a police car driven by P.C. Alfred Ventress was forced off the road and into a ford by milling sheep.

'RAM' ROVER

Both escapes had been caused by Pitts deliberately reversing his Land Rover into Mr. Abbott's wall. P.C. Rowan later found pieces of plastic from a broken car light embedded in the wall. These matched the broken rear light on Pitts' Land Rover.

After the verdict Mr. Abbott revealed that his business had been given a cash injection by a long-lost Australian relative.

THE WORLD ABOUT US

- 116 children and 28 adults were killed when a coal slag heap engulfed a school at Aberfan in Wales.

- Double agent George Blake, serving 42 years for spying, escaped from Wormwood Scrubs Prison in London.

- The latest figures put UK unemployment at 437,229 — an increase of 100,000 on September.

- The Queen granted a pardon to Timothy John Evans, hanged in 1950.

- The GPO announced that all British homes and businesses are to be given postal codes.

Ashfordly Gazette

With which is incorporated the "Ashfordly Times and North Yorkshire Advertiser"

Registered at the General Post Office as a Newspaper   Established 1856 No. 5786.   Printed and Published by HORNE & SON. LIMITED. WHITBY   FRIDAY, DECEMBER 16th, 1966.   12 Pages.   Price 3½d.   Tel. 396 (Editorial Tel. 1070)

AIDENSFIELD EDITION

THE BEST CHRISTMAS PRESENT OF ALL

— TB Boy Gets Swiss Lifeline

Lady Janet Whitly (seated, right) and P.C. Nick Rowan.

Eight-year-old tuberculosis sufferer Danny Parkin received the perfect Christmas gift this week when Lady Janet Whitly announced that she was going to pay for the boy's treatment in a Swiss sanatorium.

Lady Whitly, who lives at Whitly Hall near Aidensfield, made her generous gesture after becoming aware of the family's plight. The news brought double festive joy to the Parkins who learned that their other two children, Ellie and Ronnie, would not be prosecuted for stealing Christmas trees from Lady Whitly's estate. The brother and sister had taken the trees in the hope of raising enough money to send Danny to Switzerland.

HOME IN TIME FOR XMAS

It was on Tuesday that Danny Parkin was allowed home from hospital to spend Christmas with his family. Overhearing their jobless father saying how he wished he could afford to send Danny to Switzerland, Ellie and Ronnie hatched their illicit plan to raise cash.

Later that day Lady Whitly reported that a number of her Christmas trees had been stolen.

That evening one of the trees turned up in the bar of the Aidensfield Arms. The landlord, George Ward, told P.C. Nick Rowan that he had bought the tree from local businessman Claude Jeremiah Greengrass, 62. When P.C. Rowan examined Mr. Greengrass's truck and observed the presence of pine needles, he decided to quiz him about the matter.

SANTA TAKEN FOR QUESTIONING

At the time Mr. Greengrass was rehearsing for the village Christmas concert and was thus led off in full Santa Claus costume to be questioned at Ashfordly Police Station.

(continued on page 4)

CHRISTMAS JOY

(continued from page 1)

Mr. Greengrass protested that he knew nothing about any stolen trees and maintained that he sold the one to Mr. Ward after finding it lying in the road. His innocence was proved when Lady Whitly herself saw Ellie and Ronnie Parkin make off with another batch of trees — in the truck they had 'borrowed' from Mr. Greengrass without his knowledge. He will not be pressing charges for theft.

The stolen trees were found in the Parkins' shed.

DECK THE HALLS

The family offered Lady Whitly £5 by way of compensation and she was so touched when she heard the reason for the thefts that she agreed to drop all charges. Furthermore she announced that she would pay for Danny's treatment in Switzerland.

'It's a wonderful offer,' said family head Fred Parkin. 'It gives Danny real hope. It's made our Christmas.'

SANTA'S PLIGHT

Mr. Greengrass was less full of festive cheer. To crown a miserable week for him as Santa, he got stuck up the chimney during the Christmas concert.

Mr Greengrass (left) and Alfred, seen here smiling before their arrest.

WHAT'S ON

Saturday. Whitby Essoldo. *The Fortunes.* 7.30pm. Admission 9s 0d.

Saturday–Friday. Whitby Gaumont. *Bambi* 10.30am, 2.30pm. 'Battle of the Bulge' 6.45pm. Saturday Only: 'Georgy Girl' (X) 10pm.

Saturday–Friday. Ashfordly Regal. Christmas Double Bill. *Alfie* and *Carry On Screaming* 2pm, 6.45pm.

Wednesday. Aidensfield Village Hall. Ashfordly Townswomen's Guild Debate: Do We Really Need a Channel Tunnel? 2pm. Coffee 7d.

Thursday. The demonstration and talk on Safety In The Home And Garden due to be given by Professor Giles Penrith has had to be cancelled following his involvement in a lawn-mower accident.

GYPSY CURSE BEHIND UNDERWEAR THEFT?

Flo's gypsy encampment, not far outside the village of Aidensfield.

People Panic Over Stolen Smalls

A gypsy curse is thought to have been responsible for a number of washing line thefts in the Aidensfield area over the past week.

On Monday Gina Ward, glamorous barmaid at the Aidensfield Arms, discovered that items of underwear were missing from her washing line. They later turned up on a second-hand clothing stall at Ashfordly Market, along with two shirts and a pair of ladies' bloomers stolen from Mrs. Elsie Hardaker's clothes line.

INTIMATE GARMENTS

The thefts were subsequently traced to a gypsy known as 'Flo' who had been working the area trying to sell sprigs of so-called 'lucky heather'. It is believed that anyone who refused to buy the good luck charms ultimately paid with their washing which she then sold.

Mrs. Hardaker, of Bank Top, Aidensfield, said: 'I'm just glad to have got the stuff back. I don't like the thought of strangers with their hands all over my underwear, even if it was straight from the washing line.'

NEW DISTRICT NURSE FOR VILLAGE

Aidensfield has a new District Nurse, Maggie Bolton. She began her duties this week and says she is 'looking forward to settling down in such a beautiful part of the country.'

BABY GIRL FOR VILLAGE DOCTOR

Aidensfield's Dr. Kate Rowan gave birth to a baby girl at Ashfordly Hospital on Wednesday. The proud father, P.C. Nick Rowan, said he was thrilled but tired. He added that they intend naming the child Sarah.

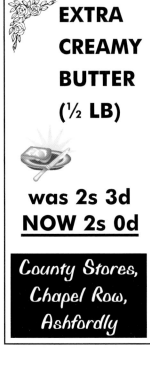

THE WORLD ABOUT US

– England football manager Alf Ramsey received a knighthood in the New Year Honours. World Cup-winning team Captain Bobby Moore was awarded an OBE.

– Speed ace Donald Campbell died when Bluebird somersaulted at 300mph during a world water speed record attempt at Coniston Water.

– *The Ken Dodd Show* was the most-watched television programme over Christmas.

– The BBC screened the first episode of a new series about a zany American beat combo called The Monkees.

Ashfordly Gazette

With which is incorporated the "Ashfordly Times and North Yorkshire Advertiser"

Registered at the General Post Office as a Newspaper | Established 1856 No. 5791. | Printed and Published by HORNE & SON, LIMITED, WHITBY | FRIDAY, JANUARY 20th, 1967. | 12 Pages. | Price 3/-d. | Tel. 396 (Editorial Tel. 1070)

AIDENSFIELD EDITION

DOCTOR LOSES FIGHT FOR LIFE

Village In Mourning For Popular Female G.P.

Kate Rowan, Aidensfield's much-loved doctor, died in the early hours of Sunday morning — just 11 days after giving birth to a baby girl, her first child. Dr. Rowan was 28.

The news stunned villagers, many of whom were unaware that Dr. Rowan was even suffering from a disease as serious as leukaemia. Her husband, P.C. Nick Rowan, was said to be 'devastated' by her death.

LOCAL BORN AND BRED

Dr. Rowan was born in nearby Eltering but went to London University in order to study medicine. In 1961 she married the young policeman and three years ago she returned to her roots when he was transferred to Aidensfield from the Metropolitan Police. She became a partner in the Aidensfield practice of Dr. Alex Ferrenby, her childhood mentor, and took over when Dr. Ferrenby died in 1965. At one time she combined her duties in Aidensfield with a partnership in Whitby.

It is thought that even her husband did not know the extent of her illness until their baby was born.

P.C. Nick Rowan (second from left), husband of the deceased, at the funeral of his beloved wife.

TESTS SHOWED DOCTOR KNEW

A spokesman for Ashfordly Hospital said: 'A blood test early on in the pregnancy showed that she was anaemic but she said that she would treat it herself. The District Nurse was so worried about how pale Dr. Rowan looked that she made her have another test at 36 weeks. But Dr. Rowan sent that one off under another name and kept the results to herself. When the results came through, they showed that she had acute leukaemia. It was only then that she told those closest to her that she was seriously ill.'

(continued on page 2)

SPECIAL NOTICE

Through the pages of the *Gazette* P.C. Nick Rowan would like to thank everyone for their kind words and deeds over the past week.

P.C. Nick Rowan holds his two-week-old daughter.

DOCTOR DEATH

(continued from page 1)

Dr. Rowan was released from hospital on 6 January and initially responded well to treatment but three nights later, after a drive with her husband and baby up to her favourite beauty spot at Cloud End, she developed a temperature of 103. Doctors diagnosed that pneumonia had set in.

TOO LITTLE, TOO LATE

Despite taking antibiotics, her condition worsened and she passed away shortly after 3.30 on Sunday morning.

Her funeral took place at Aidensfield Church on Wednesday with the entire village turning out to pay tribute. Sgt. Oscar Blaketon, P.C. Rowan's superior officer, said: 'She was a fine woman, a first-rate doctor and a caring wife. It's tragic that something like this should happen to someone with her whole life ahead of her. The sympathies of everyone on the North Riding force go out to P.C. Rowan.'

POPULAR FIGURE

Local character Claude Jeremiah Greengrass, 65, spoke for the whole community when he added: 'You'd never hear anyone say a bad word about Dr. Rowan. Her husband, maybe. But her, never.'

It is understood that P.C. Rowan is planning to have his newly-born daughter christened Katie, rather than Sarah, in memory of his late wife.

THE WORLD ABOUT US

– The government announced the construction of a new town to cover 22,000 acres of rural Buckinghamshire. It is to be called Milton Keynes.

– Jo Grimond was succeeded by Old Etonian Jeremy Thorpe as leader of the Liberal Party.

– After 88 years in circulation, the *Boys' Own Paper* closed down. It blamed 'market changes' for its demise.

– The Monkees — straight after their TV success — went to the top of the hit parade with 'I'm a Believer'.

WOMAN DIES IN HOUSE BLAZE

— Teacher Husband Arrested

A local schoolteacher was in police custody last night suspected of killing his wife and then setting their house on fire.

Barry Jackson, a teacher at Aidensfield Village School, was arrested following the suspicious death of his wife Sophie on Saturday night. Firemen found her dead in the bedroom of their burnt-out house in Upper Mill Lane. The fire had been started deliberately.

MENTAL PROBLEMS

Mrs. Jackson was known to have been suffering from a form of mental illness which affected her behaviour and memory. Four days before her death she sustained minor injuries after crashing her car into a bus shelter and narrowly missing a group of schoolchildren. It was her third traffic offence in the space of 15 minutes. On an earlier occasion local man Claude Jeremiah Greengrass, 73, had been forced to dive into a ditch to avoid her oncoming car. He was said to be demanding a new suit and boots by way of compensation. Mrs. Jackson had also been accused of stealing from a local shop.

HATE CAMPAIGN?

Mrs. Jackson's irrational behaviour alarmed some villagers and her husband told the police that he had received an anonymous typewritten poison pen letter. Their house was also daubed with the slogan 'Lock her up'.

Then shortly after 10.30 on Saturday night, District Nurse Maggie Bolton raised the alarm that the Jacksons' house was on fire. P.C. Nick

P.C. Alfred Ventress captured by a *Gazette* photographer sighting a suspected UFO (story on page 7).

Rowan was first on the scene, closely followed by Mr. Jackson who revealed that his wife was inside. P.C. Rowan had difficulty in preventing Mr. Jackson from dashing into the burning house. Firemen beat back the flames but found Mrs. Jackson's body in a bedroom.
(continued on page 7)

FIRE ARREST
(continued from page 6)

While fire crews mopped up, they found evidence which suggested arson. The police realised that they could be dealing with a murder inquiry.

Mr. Jackson had previously denied having anything to do with the poison pen letter, claiming that, apart from anything else, he could not type. However P.C. Nick Rowan found evidence to the contrary and was able to match the print on Mr. Jackson's typewriter with that on the letter.

MR. JACKSON'S BREAKDOWN

On Wednesday P.C. Rowan again confronted Mr. Jackson about the letter. According to unconfirmed reports, he broke down and said that his wife had begged him to end her life because she realised that she was losing her mind. So he allegedly sent the malicious letter and painted the slogans to absolve himself of suspicion and then suffocated her before setting fire to the house.

He is expected to be charged over the weekend.

The 'flying saucer' gives a nasty fright to Mr. Claude Jeremiah Greengrass.

MULTIPLE UFO SIGHTING DURING STORM

Three separate sightings of a possible 'flying saucer' were reported at the height of a violent storm which rocked Aidensfield on Monday.

P.C. Alfred Ventress of Ashfordly Police told colleagues that he had been dazzled by a bright light whilst parking his car near the golf course. The glare caused him to hit his head on the car windscreen. When District Nurse Maggie Bolton examined him for concussion, she noticed that one side of his face appeared sunburnt.

Later P.C. Ventress and P.C. Nick Rowan visited the spot where the light had been seen and found a patch of dry ground among the puddles.

POLICE CURIOUS

'It's all a bit weird,' admitted P.C. Rowan. 'Alf was adamant about what he had seen and two other witnesses — Luke Halliwell and old Claude Greengrass — also said they'd seen a UFO land on the golf course during the storm. It makes you wonder.'

POLICE SCEPTICAL

Sgt. Oscar Blaketon of Ashfordly Police remained unconvinced. 'I think that bump on the head has made Ventress talk more rubbish than usual.'

'BERO MAN' SENSATION— MASKED BURGLAR WAS TEENAGE GIRL

'Desired Excitement' — Court Told

An Aidensfield girl was today beginning a 12-month custodial sentence after being sent to borstal for a string of burglaries which terrorised her home village.

Over a three-week period in January the burglar, face-masked by a white flour bag with eye holes, struck with such frequency that house-holders in the district slept with their lights on. Some farmers kept shotguns by the side of their beds. Little did they know that the notorious intruder nicknamed 'Bero Man' on account of the Bero flour bag worn as a mask was really a 15-year-old girl, Marion Flax.

ATTRACTIVE VICTIM

Among the burglar's victims was Gina Ward, lovely barmaid of the Aidensfield Arms. She was disturbed at night in her bedroom but the raider ran off when Miss Ward's uncle, landlord George Ward, came to her rescue.

The police were then called to a break-in at Flax Farm where Marion Flax said she had been confronted by 'Bero Man'. She claimed that he ran off when she screamed. However she was the only witness to the incident. Later that same day, 'Bero Man' was seen dancing on a distant burial ground while emergency crews attended a car crash.

The robber struck next at the home of local business-man Claude Jeremiah Greengrass, 59, narrowly evading capture. Not surprisingly, the thief managed to outpace Mr. Greengrass.

A JOB TOO FAR

The final burglary was at the home of District Nurse Maggie Bolton. Returning from work at Ashfordly Hospital, she came face to face with 'Bero Man'. The ensuing struggle left her winded and dazed, enabling the culprit to make a success-ful escape.

With the only description of 'Bero Man' being that he was young and stocky, police had little to go on until P.C. Nick Rowan, in the course of routine inquiries, visited the home of Mr. Greengrass. On the kitchen wall he noticed a clock which had been stolen in the raid on Flax Farm. Mr. Greengrass said that he had bought the clock and other items from Marion Flax.

(continued on page 8)

Sgt. Oscar Blaketon (right) quizzes 'Bero Man' suspect Jason Rickards.

An innocent man: Jason Rickards with Miss Gina Ward.

THE WORLD ABOUT US

– The Torrey Canyon oil tanker ran aground off Land's End and began spilling thousands of tons of oil.

– Petrol companies announced the introduction of a star-grading system.

– 65-year-old yachtsman Francis Chichester rounded Cape Horn on the last leg of his solo voyage around the world.

EVENING CANCELLED

A special evening with TV Memory Man Cedric Wilkinson, scheduled for Aidensfield Village Hall on Monday, was cancelled when he forgot to turn up.

GIRL BURGLAR

(continued from page 2)

P.C. Rowan set off for Flax Farm and arrived to find Maggie Bolton, on a call to treat Mr. Flax, cornered by 'Bero Man'. The burglar made a run for it but any escape was blocked by the appearance of Mr. Flax levelling a shotgun. It was than that 'Bero Man' removed the mask to reveal her true identity.

OUT OF TOUCH

In mitigation, Lesley Henderson, for Marion Flax, told Ashfordly Juvenile Court that the defendant had low self-esteem and few friends. 'Because of her rounded build, she feels that she is not physically attractive and cannot wear the latest fashions,' said Miss Henderson. 'Her father, although essentially a well-meaning man, is from a different generation and totally out of tune with the needs and tastes of a teenage girl. The house has barely made it into the Fifties, let alone the Sixties.

'As a result, Marion Flax felt trapped in a lonely existence. She desperately wanted Maggie Bolton, the District Nurse, to be her friend because she found it difficult to mix. Her criminal actions were partly a desire for excitement and partly a cry for help. She felt that she might as well be in a real prison as spend the rest of her life at Flax Farm.'

THE STORY OF HEARTBEAT

In this special eight-page colour pull-out, using the latest printing technology, we talk to the stars and the producers of the popular television series *Heartbeat* which is filmed in our area.

Now in its ninth successful series, *Heartbeat* is the highest-rated UK drama with viewing figures constantly topping the 17 million mark. It is a worldwide phenomenon, having been sold to 36 countries. Yet its origins lie in a relatively obscure series of novels written by North Yorkshire country policeman Peter Walker under the pen-name of Nicholas Rhea. Set in the 1960s, the *Constable* books as they were called had been under option for some time before being brought to the attention of Yorkshire Television, who recognised the potential for a hit series.

Executive producer Keith Richardson, the Controller of Drama for Yorkshire Television, says: 'We had been in Hong Kong doing the series *Yellowthread Street* and thought we'd better do something closer to home. In the *Constable* books the wife was at the kitchen sink but we made her a doctor so that we had a police and a medical story. In a smallish community, the two would intertwine. This gave us a two-pronged story — either he could solve the crime or she could, by looking up medical records. And from that we took our title *Heartbeat* — the 'heart' representing the medical side and the 'beat' referring to the policeman's beat.

'The real key to the show's success was the casting in the first instance. Nick Berry, who played Nick Rowan, and Niamh Cusack, who played his wife Kate, were very different individuals offscreen but onscreen they just had a chemistry. It was also brave in terms of TV wanting to present a couple who had a successful marriage. For 8p.m. on a Sunday it's quite nice to see two people who like each other.

'Then there was the setting. The show's first producer, Stuart Doughty, and I looked around various places to film and obviously wanted to find somewhere reasonably close to our base in Leeds. But we couldn't find anywhere with the right feel. Then we came across Goathland up on the North York Moors which not only has an extraordinary feel to it, but it has the added bonus of the railway. So Goathland became our Aidensfield.

'When we'd finished shooting the first series, we looked at it and thought there isn't any real sense of period, partly because Goathland is unaltered for 100 years, Yorkshire farmers are not the snappiest dressers in the world so there was no sense of Sixties fashions, and they still drive old Triumph Heralds.'

Keith Richardson, Executive Producer

Gerry Mill, Producer

'So we put the music on to say, "Hey, this is the Sixties." The music has helped to bring the generations together to watch the programme. You've got mums and dads bouncing around on the sofa remembering the songs and you've got teenagers who are just discovering Sixties music.

'When Niamh said she was leaving, it was a big blow but by giving her a heroine's death and with the audience wondering how Nick was going to cope, we were able to reach new heights.

'We introduced Mike Bradley seven episodes before Nick Berry left and made him a different kind of character. We had a short-list of six for Nick's replacement but I wanted Jason Durr for the

part. We had a test — anybody who could wear that policeman's motorcycle helmet and look good got the job!'

Producer Gerry Mill attributes the success of *Heartbeat* to the fact that it is 'good old-fashioned family entertainment with plenty of nostalgia and no sex or violence. It is drama with human interest. Since Dr. Bolton was killed, we haven't had a doctor but with solicitor Jackie Lambert, we've now got both sides of the law. Jackie conflicts with Craddock and conflicts make good drama.

'One of the real stars of the show is North Yorkshire itself. I think viewers who live in cities love to look at the spectacular scenery so I tell directors: "Get as many

shots of the moors as you can between the snow showers…"

'It's amazing the number of Australians we get turning up to watch filming on wet nights in North Yorkshire. The show is huge in Australia — I think it reminds them of how Britain used to be.'

The producers have tried to remain as faithful to the Sixties period as possible but Keith Richardson admits that they have occasionally taken liberties. 'For example when Kate was dying we used the song 'Time in a Bottle' even though it wasn't actually recorded until 1974. My story is that Jim Croce wrote it in 1968!

'Initially we kept giving Niamh a beehive hairstyle because it was right for 1964. She went through the first

ten episodes looking spectacularly awful so we glammed her up for the second series.

'We don't get many complaints but we did get a letter from a viewer regarding a Land Rover in one episode. He said that it was spot on for the period but the tyres were modern. I wrote back saying that under the Health and Safety Act we would have problems with actors driving around on 30-year-old tyres! Another episode was about Foot-and-Mouth disease and contained a shot of a dead cow hanging there. We had to assure people that no animals were killed or burned in the making of the episode … nor did the actor who appeared to have committed suicide actually kill himself.'

JASON DURR as P.C. MIKE BRADLEY

Jason Durr is in his element riding a motorcycle across the North York Moors while patrolling Mike Bradley's beat. 'When you stand there on a sunny day,' says 32-year-old Jason, 'and look out across the moors, you couldn't ask for more. I ride a motorbike anyway and to ride across the moors is just great. It's all so peaceful. I must admit sometimes I pretend I can't hear the walkie-talkie with the crew's instructions at the end of a take and I just carry on riding off into the sunset for a minute or two rather than return immediately for the next take!

'From doing *Heartbeat*, Triumph Motorcycles UK asked me whether I would like a bike of my own. So now I've got a Triumph Bonneville. They're fantastic bikes — it's a perk of the job.'

Jason confesses that prior to landing the plum role as *Heartbeat*'s young male lead in succession to Nick Berry, he hadn't seen much of the show. 'I'd only watched a couple of episodes but at least that gave me an idea of what the show was about. I'm actually quite glad I hadn't seen too many episodes because I think it might have clouded my opinion and there was always the danger that I might have tried to make Mike too much like Nick Rowan. As it was, I was able to come to the show with a fresh viewpoint.

'Mike's a good contrast to Nick. He's a bit of an action man and likes to live fast — if you can live fast in Aidensfield! Somehow I can't see him turning into Alf Ventress as he gets older. He's conscientious, he takes his job seriously but he likes to follow hunches and he's also got a lighter side.'

Did Jason feel daunted about taking over from Nick Berry? 'Nick was a tough act to follow,' says Jason. 'When a show's a big success — and Nick was a huge success in it — it can be difficult, but nobody ever put any pressure on me. I never felt that the burden was riding on my shoulders. Nevertheless, it was something of a relief when the viewing figures actually went up after I had joined ... even though I'm sure it was nothing to do with me.'

Modesty aside, Jason, who is married to Janine Ruby, singer with the band Trifecta, says he receives a lot of fan mail. 'It's nice to know that the public appreciate what you're doing. I had a letter once from a lady whose daughter is blind and she listens to the show and derives a great deal of pleasure from it. For me, that was extremely rewarding.

'I think the reason *Heartbeat* has been so successful is that people know they're going to be watching a gentle hour of drama where they won't get pummelled with violence or bad language. There is a place for hard-hitting shows but you can get weary of too much violence, both in drama and on the news. I like to think we can send viewers off to work on a Monday morning with a smile on their face.'

Jason was raised in Hong Kong and acquired the acting bug after appearing in a number of shows at school there. His father was also keen on amateur dramatics. 'I remember doing "Joseph and His Amazing Technicolour Dreamcoat" at school in Hong Kong when I was about eight.

At the time I was also helping my dad paint the scenery for an amateur production he was doing and I managed to miss the first performance of the school play. I was relegated from Joseph to third donkey on the left because I had forgotten to turn up. I learned my lesson ...'

Since leaving drama school in London, Jason has appeared in Royal Shakespeare Company productions of 'Macbeth' (he played Malcolm), 'Measure For Measure' and 'The Blue Angel' and in TV series such as *The Paradise Club*, *The Chief*, *Inspector Morse*, *Sharpe's Battle* and *Bugs*.

'Until Mike Bradley, I had usually played antagonists in trouble with the law so this was a change of direction for me. But when we're filming in Goathland, I chat to the police who were around in the 1960s and they give me an insight into what the job was like in those days. In particular they tell you how boring all the paperwork was. They give me tips and sometimes I can incorporate those ideas into the part. Playing a policeman is really an ongoing learning process for me.'

BILL MAYNARD as
CLAUDE JEREMIAH GREENGRASS

Bill Maynard says this will probably be his last series as loveable rogue Claude Jeremiah Greengrass, the bane of the North Riding Police. 'I've done nine years in *Heartbeat* and I think I've taken the character about as far as I can. The time has come for a change, to do something different. I was going to leave a couple of years back but because Nick Berry left, there was such a brouhaha about whether or not the show would survive without him. So I stayed on because I wanted to prove that it would. And it has.'

At 70, Bill has enjoyed an illustrious showbusiness career spanning nearly half a century. Yet his ultimate goal was to be a professional footballer. 'I was on Leicester City's books but I got divided cruciates at 16 so that ended that. But even as a child I'd always been a bit of a performer — doing George Formby impressions — so I followed that course and joined Butlin's as a singer with the band. And it all took off from there. I've been on TV for 46 years now. In the Fifties I did three series with Terry Scott called *Great Scott — It's Maynard!*, I had the Sixties out, in the Seventies I had top-rating comedy shows like *The Life Of Riley* and *Oh No — It's Selwyn Froggitt*, in the Eighties there were three series of *The Gaffer* and in the Nineties, *Heartbeat*.

'I've never stopped working. I went skint in the Sixties but one of the reasons for that was that I went from variety and TV to doing repertory work. I went from £1,000 a week to £50 a week.

'People still call me Selwyn and put their thumbs up and say "Magic". You can tell how old people are by what they call you — the kids call me "Greengrass", the older ones say "Selwyn".

'I feel a tremendous responsibility to the public and if something's being done which the public won't understand or is unfunny, I'll fight tooth and nail to get it put right. It doesn't necessarily endear me to a lot of people but it's the way I've always worked. I admit I'm arrogant and bloody-minded and, to a lot of people, I'm a complete pain in the arse. But I'm a professional. Yorkshire Television have been very good to me which is why *Heartbeat* is the best job I've ever had in television.'

Yet the role of Greengrass marked something of a departure for Bill. 'I normally play the lead character but this was different. Yorkshire [TV] rang up and said, "It's not the lead, but we want you to come in and see if you can do something with this character, and they pretty much gave me carte blanche to change it around and make it work.

'I had a picture in my mind of how Greengrass should look and speak. I had to make him a loveable rogue. It was first mooted that he should wear a black crombie but I thought it was too sombre. Instead I wanted to wear an army greatcoat because I feel that a rogue would wear one to make out that he'd been in the army. They wanted him to wear a cap, but I said a trilby and I added the neckerchief and mittens. I'd been given Greengrass' boots when I appeared in the 1972 film *Adolf Hitler — My Part In His Downfall* by Spike Milligan. I've played a lot of army parts in films and every time you turn up, they give you a brand new pair of boots. It always takes until the end of filming to get them to feel right but this pair fitted like gloves so I bought them for £2 at the end of the shoot. And I wore them through *Selwyn Froggitt*, *The Gaffer*, other films and the first few years of *Heartbeat*. It

was only then that the soles finally went.

'Then there are his mannerisms. I used to play golf with a bloke who was a builder and whenever he used to cheat a bit, he twitched. It was a dead giveaway. So I gave Greengrass a twitch so that the audience would know when he was telling lies. I've also given Greengrass expressions like "Don't do that, I'm nearly an old age pensioner", which I had always used as Bill Maynard. I pick up phrases from people I meet and store them in my memory bank ready to trot them out in the programme. Greengrass doesn't say "No", he says "And pigs

might …" And instead of "Yes", he says "Can a duck … ?" They're his catchphrases.

'Greengrass has changed slightly now that he's got two sidekicks in Bernie Scripps and David. Because you couldn't have three weak characters, Claude has become the leader and is now more worldly and articulate. I reckon at some stage he was a professional man — a bank manager or a doctor — before deciding to opt out. That's why he is articulate. One thing's for certain — the public seem to like him. And I'm thrilled by that because they are the people who matter.'

DEREK FOWLDS as OSCAR BLAKETON

Derek Fowlds confesses that he very nearly turned down the role of Oscar Blaketon in *Heartbeat*.

'I'd just done an episode of *The Darling Buds Of May* for Yorkshire playing a drunken ventriloquist,' remembers London-born Derek. 'I was having dinner with my agent and the *Heartbeat* casting director Malcolm Drury was also there and talking about this new series. But I almost talked myself out of it. After reading the script, I phoned my agent and said, "I'm a bit old to play Nick." I thought it must be Nick they wanted me to play because he was the only southerner in it. But my agent said, "No, they want you to play the gruff, north country sergeant" … which made him all the things I'm not. I really wasn't sure whether I was right for it but I decided that since it was only for six episodes, I'd give it a go. And here I am nine series later …'

Derek then had to find the right look for Blaketon. 'In the books Greengrass is a little weasel of a man and Blaketon is big so I think Bill Maynard and I could have played each other's parts. But I decided to base Blaketon on Corporal Maund, my old drill instructor in National Service who used to delight in putting his face in mine and calling me a horrible little man. So I cut my hair very short, greased it back and shouted a lot. Dear old Corporal Maund ended up inadvertently doing me a favour because he was obviously just right for a Sixties police sergeant. In fact I've had a lot of letters from ex-policemen saying they had a sergeant just like him. It seems every station had a Blaketon back then.'

Derek reckons that Blaketon served in the army before joining the police force. 'He is a strict disciplinarian as a result of his army career and he ran Ashfordly Police Station like he ran his platoon in the army.'

'He didn't settle at the Post Office and when he came into money from an old aunt, he decided to take over the Aidensfield Arms ... although he'd like to change the name to the Blaketon Arms. And he's still policing the community in his own way from behind the bar. It's that thing about once a copper, always a copper.

'He thinks Craddock, his successor as station sergeant, is a complete pillock and never misses an opportunity to undermine his authority. This he does by regularly going back to the station to visit "his lads". But he does genuinely miss them because there is a surprising warmth to Blaketon deep down. I did try to introduce a skeleton into Blaketon's cupboard whereby he changed into women's clothes and on Sundays became a transvestite known as Olive but the powers-that-be didn't fancy the idea!'

Few actors have enjoyed such a diverse career as Derek who has managed to combine serious drama (*Edward the Seventh*, *Clayhanger*, *Casualty*) with comedy (*Yes, Minister*, *Agony*, *Doctor in Distress*) and being straight man to a puppet fox. 'I was sidekick to Basil Brush from 1969 to 1974 and we did eight series and three Royal Command Performances. Morecambe and Wise used to say to us: "Stop pinching our act!" I loved working with Basil and I miss him to this day. But my time with him is not forgotten. I still get called "Mr. Derek" in the street and I still get a Christmas card from Ivan Owen who created him.

'It's funny, this is my 39th year as an actor but a lot of people think I've only done three jobs — Basil Brush, *Yes, Minister* and *Heartbeat*. Yet I've played so many roles because acting to me has been about playing different people. I wouldn't know how to play myself.

'I landed the part of Bernard in *Yes, Minister* after my agent, who also looked after Jonathan Lynn, the co-writer, recommended me.

She told me: "You're going to get a script called *Yes, Minister*." I thought it was about vicars. I was 52 when I did that and Bernard was meant to be 36.

'So on the face of it I was just as unsuitable to play him as I was to play Blaketon. But in both cases I seem to have made it work.'

GOOSEBERRY FOOLS

—Wife The Culprit As Fruit Show Is Ruined

Hector and Anthea Cowley pictured at Aidensfield Show.

A bitter sabotage dispute between two rival entrants in the gooseberry competition at the annual Aidensfield Show was finally defused when the real culprit turned out to be the wife of one of the protagonists.

Local grower Claude Jeremiah Greengrass, 66, locked horns with Aidensfield's newly-appointed Special Constable, Hector Cowley, over who had the best fruit. Both men were determined to win the coveted first prize but their zeal spilled over into open warfare when Mr. Cowley discovered that his prize specimens had been trampled underfoot — on the day before the show.

GOOSEBERRY CRUSH

Utilising his detective know-how, Mr. Cowley realised that he had a vital piece of evidence — a neckerchief which had been left behind at the scene of the crime. Also aware that it belonged to Mr. Greengrass, he proceeded to arrest him at Saturday's show on a charge of gooseberry-wrecking.

FRUITY WIFE

As Mr. Cowley prepared to lead his rival off to Ashfordly Police Station in full view of the stunned summer crowds, Mr. Greengrass protested his innocence. 'I admit I went to his garden to spy on his fruit and that's when I must have dropped my neckerchief. But I never trampled on his blasted gooseberries.'

Mr. Cowley was suitably unimpressed but the wind was taken out of his sails when his wife Anthea suddenly came forward and confessed that she was to blame. She said she was fed up with taking second place to her husband's fruit fetish.

CONFUSION

Mr. Greengrass's joy was short-lived. For his dubious tactics resulted in his disqualification from the competition. Afterwards he stormed: 'I shall be writing to this new Omnibusman or whatever his name is.'

THE WORLD ABOUT US

– Glasgow Celtic triumphed in the final of the European Cup — the first British team to win the competition.

– Francis Chichester aboard *Gipsy Moth IV* arrived in Plymouth at the end of his epic round-the-world solo voyage.

– The Beatles released their latest LP, *Sergeant Pepper's Lonely Hearts Club Band*. It has been described as a 'concept album'.

Ashfordly Gazette

With which is incorporated the "Ashfordly Times and North Yorkshire Advertiser"

Registered at the General Post Office as a Newspaper — Established 1856 No. 5815. — Printed and Published by HORNE & SON. LIMITED. WHITBY — FRIDAY, JUNE 16th, 1967. — 12 Pages. — Price 3½d. — Tel. 396 (Editorial Tel. 1070)

AIDENSFIELD EDITION

WORLD WAR TWO BOMB BLAST SHATTERS AIDENSFIELD

Man Killed, Houses Destroyed

'A Scene Of Utter Devastation' —

Claude Jeremiah Greengrass (below, right) discovered the bomb — in a somewhat unconventional manner.

The calm of a summer's afternoon in Aidensfield was shattered in horrific circumstances on Wednesday when a huge German war bomb exploded in Ash Lane. One man — a member of the bomb disposal team — was killed by the blast and several buildings in the vicinity were badly damaged.

'It was a scene of utter devastation,' said one witness. 'It is a miracle more people weren't injured.'

EMERGENCY EVACUATION

The explosion occurred at 2.14pm as members of the Royal Engineers' Bomb Disposal Unit set about disarming the device which had been uncovered by a mechanical digger. The area was evacuated while the three-man team tackled the highly unstable bomb.

(continued on page 2)

All Emergency Services were present as the local area was evacuated.

BOMB BLAST

(continued from page 1)

With the explosive starting to decompose, the bomb became increasingly dangerous and the team had to remove the chemicals by hand. Two of their number were overcome by fumes, leaving Sapper Terence Smith, a married man from Colchester in Essex, to soldier on alone. Then without warning, the bomb suddenly went off. Sapper Smith was killed instantly.

The blast, which could be heard ten miles away, caused extensive damage to nearby properties. Worst hit was the house of Aidensfield station-master Bob Hutton which was reduced to a pile of rubble. His garden shed was also destroyed.

LUCKY P.C. FINDS MISSING BOY

At the time of the explosion, P.C. Nick Rowan was searching Mr. Hutton's garden for a 12-year-old school-boy, Colin Ellis, who had been reported missing. Rescue teams dug frantically in the rubble and happily found P.C. Rowan and the boy unharmed.

Afterwards P.C. Rowan told the *Gazette*: 'It all happened so suddenly. I remember hearing a noise in Mr. Hutton's garden shed, but it was locked. I managed to climb in and there I found Colin. The next thing there was this terrific bang and the building collapsed around us. I guess we're lucky to be alive.'

ONGOING CRISIS

Emergency teams were still clearing the damage throughout Wednesday night and Thursday morning. Those unlucky enough to have homes damaged or destroyed spent the night at St. Mark's Convent in Ashfordly while others sim-

ply counted their blessings.

Yet Wednesday had dawned like any other day in what has always been a haven of rural tranquility. Among those going about their business in the village was P.C. Alfred Ventress of Ashfordly Police who had purchased a plot of land in Ash Lane with a view to having a retirement bungalow built there. With hindsight, perhaps his first mistake was employing the services of local handyman Claude Jeremiah Greengrass, 61.

(continued on page 5)

The noise of the bomb blast was heard up to ten miles away.

VILLAGE EXPLOSION

P.C. Nick Rowan (right) with Colin Ellis, the missing schoolboy.

(continued from page 2)

'Claude had offered to dig me a cesspit,' lamented P.C. Ventress yesterday. 'I was expecting him to come along with something that was state-of-the-art but the digger he turned up with was more like state-of-the-Ark. It was old and rusty and somehow I knew there would be problems.

'Sure enough after an hour or so, the digger hit some kind of obstruction and Claude climbed down from the cab to investigate. His assistant — a lad called David Stockwell who's not the brightest — tried to move the digger but the bucket fell into the pit ... right on top of Claude.'

DANGER — UXB

Trapped and therefore unable to move, Mr. Greengrass realised to his horror that he was face-to-face with an unexploded wartime bomb. 'I'm not often lost for words, me,' he said later. 'but this time I could hardly bring myself to say the word "bomb".'

P.C. Rowan was riding past when he was flagged down by David Stockwell. Told about the bomb, P.C. Rowan radioed to Ashfordly for the Bomb Squad to be brought in. He immediately set about evacuating the area, including the children from the nearby school.

HEAVYWEIGHT

Within 20 minutes Ashfordly Fire Brigade were on the scene, eventually followed by the three-man Bomb Disposal Unit who began the delicate task of winching Mr. Greengrass off the bomb.

(continued on page 6)

BOMB DRAMA

(continued from page 5)

The exercise required their strongest equipment.

Covered in mud, Mr. Greengrass was then taken by train to St. Mark's Convent for a much-needed bath. Two nuns had to be treated for shock.

SOLDIER KILLED

Shortly after Mr. Greengrass' removal, the bomb began ticking ominously. The army team knew that it could go off at any minute. Tragically for Sapper Smith, it did precisely that. When the dust settled, the site of P.C. Ventress's planned retirement home was a 30ft.-wide crater. Afterwards Mr. Greengrass played down the heroic role that he played in the afternoon's events. 'No, you shouldn't call me a hero,' he said. 'But if you insist, make sure you get my age right for once. I'm 61.'

PARALLELS

Over the past two weeks, most of us have witnessed scenes of devastation on our television screens with coverage of the Arab-Israeli Six-Day War. None of us could have imagined we would ever see such horrors on our own doorstep.

MYSTERY OF BODY FOUND IN HOUSE

P.C. Phil Bellamy and Sgt. Oscar Blaketon (hands on hips) survey the ruins.

Last night it emerged that the Aidensfield bomb blast had indirectly claimed a second casualty — a man in his forties.

While P.C. Nick Rowan was searching for missing schoolboy Colin Ellis, he and the boy's mother had cause to enter the house of Aidensfield station-master Bob Hutton. In an upstairs bedroom, they discovered a man's body. Mr. Hutton was also in the house, in a highly-distressed state.

The talk of the chattering classes was that Mr. Hutton's wife, Sandra, had an illicit lover, causing police to believe that the man had been the victim of a crime of passion.

DIED IN BED — 'AWAKE'

They were contemplating bringing murder charges against Mr. Hutton until last night a suitably shamed Mrs. Hutton revealed that the deceased was indeed her paramour but that he had died of a heart attack.

According to Mrs. Hutton he suffered from a weak heart anyway and, fearing that their affair had been uncovered when she was evacuated from the house during the bomb scare, he collapsed on the spot.

As condemnation of Mrs. Hutton's wanton behaviour echoed through Aidensfield in the wake of the disclosure, she was believed to be preparing to move to another part of the country.

The dead man has not been named until next of kin have been informed.

ST. COLUMBA'S TREASURE: FOUND AND LOST

— Valuable Archive Burned For Warmth By Sergeant And Large Part-Time Archaeologist

The ancient treasure of St. Columba's Abbey was finally unearthed this week ... but only after it had been reduced to a pile of ashes.

The accident, described as 'a monumental blunder' by one expert, occurred after two men had become trapped in a tunnel beneath the abbey ruins. Desperate to keep warm, one of the pair — part-time archaeologist Claude Jeremiah Greengrass — lit a fire with what appeared to be a pile of old documents, unaware that they formed the priceless contents of the secret abbey library.

TREASURE HUNT

Stories of a hidden treasure in St. Columba's have been circulating for years but intensified following the recent death of noted archaeologist Professor Hugo Brigstocke who lived close to the ruins. The word was that he had kept quiet about certain items which he had excavated from the abbey.

Hot on the treasure trial was Mr. Greengrass who, on Monday afternoon, was seen entering a tunnel at the abbey by Sgt. Oscar Blaketon of Ashfordly Police. Sgt. Blaketon was keen to talk to Mr. Greengrass about the recent theft of a number of

Mr. Greengrass (left) and Sgt. Blaketon — trapped in the tunnel.

trout from Ashfordly Hall.

STUCK FAST

Sgt. Blaketon followed his quarry into the tunnel but Mr. Greengrass unwittingly triggered a rockfall which blocked their exit. They pressed ahead in the hope of finding another escape route before Sgt. Blaketon was injured when the floor gave way beneath his feet.

(continued on page 8)

DOCUMENTS DESTROYED

(continued from page 2)

While Sgt. Blaketon rested, Mr. Greengrass hunted around in the hope of finding the treasure and thought he had struck gold when he located a series of tin chests. But to his dismay they contained only old Latin manuscripts.

SURVIVAL

As the damp in the tunnel began to take hold, Mr. Greengrass decided to burn these apparently worthless books so that he and Sgt. Blaketon could keep warm. It was only when the two men were rescued by P.C. Rowan via another entrance to the ruins from Professor Brigstocke's library that they realised they had set fire to the St. Columba's treasure.

INVALUABLE

Told that the documents were 'priceless', Mr. Greengrass commented: 'Oh that's all right then.' It was then pointed out to him that 'priceless' was not the same as 'worthless'.

PIRATE RADIO MENACE

Complaints from Aidensfield folk flooded in to the *Gazette* this week after they were unable to listen to their favourite radio programmes. Instead of 'Woman's Hour' and 'The Clitheroe Kid', listeners found themselves bombarded with loud popular music.

OPINION

Seth Clayton of Hawkrigg Farm moaned: 'I tuned in to the Tuesday episode of "The Archers" but all I could get was some rubbish by some beat group calling themselves The Herd. I tell you, my herd could do better!'

The pop invasion is thought to have been the result of an illegal pirate radio station conducting test transmissions off the coast. Ashfordly Police are investigating.

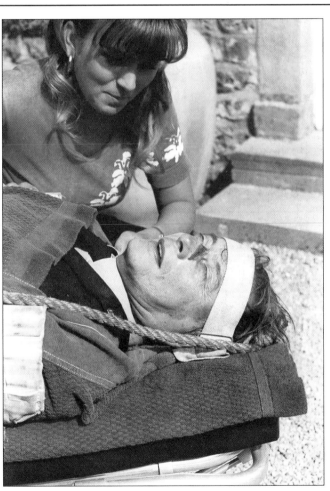

Sgt. Blaketon is taken to hospital on a stretcher.

THE WORLD ABOUT US

– Britain's first cash-dispensing machine was opened at Barclays Bank in Enfield, Middlesex.

– Rolling Stones Keith Richard and Mick Jagger were jailed for drugs offences.

– Hollywood actress Jayne Mansfield has died, aged 35.

WOMAN IN COMA AFTER HIT-AND-RUN

— District Nurse Cleared Of Blame

Susan Watkins of Moor End Cottage, Aidensfield, was still in a coma yesterday three days after being knocked off her bicycle by a hit and run driver. Last night a local man — Michael Harvey — was being questioned by police at Ashfordly.

Miss Watkins, who worked for Mr. Harvey, was found lying in the middle of the Elsinby road with head injuries by District Nurse Maggie Bolton. The damaged nature of Mrs. Bolton's car led police to believe that she may have been involved in the accident. However she claimed that she herself had been forced off the road by another car.

RIGHT NURSE, WRONG CAR

An unpleasant whispering campaign started against the popular nurse but her name was cleared when paint samples from her car did not match those at the scene of the crime.

Meanwhile investigations revealed that Michael Harvey, a man prone to blackouts, had proposed marriage to Miss Watkins on the evening of the crash and that his son, Ronald, was also having an intimate relationship with her. Ronald Harvey told the police that he had found his father at the end of the drive to their house on Monday evening. He said his father had suffered one of his blackouts.

P.C. Nick Rowan checked both of the Harveys' cars and found the pair of them to be in pristine condition. But he then discovered that Michael Harvey owned a third car — a Riley. As the search for the missing car was stepped up,

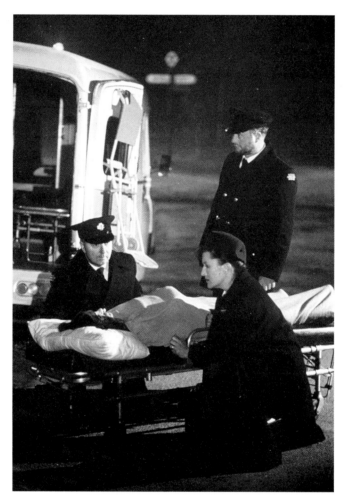

District Nurse Maggie Bolton comforts hit-and-run victim Susan Watkins.

Michael Harvey turned himself in to the police and admitted that it was he who was responsible for Miss Watkins' accident.

MISSING CAR DISCOVERED

He added that the car was hidden in his barn. There officers found the damaged Riley. Next to it were the remains of Miss Watkins' bicycle.

Mr. Harvey is expected to be charged later today.

SON CHARGED WITH HIT AND RUN

In a surprise development, Ashfordly Police have charged local man Ronald Harvey over the hit-and-run case which left his girlfriend Susan Watkins in a coma. Miss Watkins suffered severe head injuries after being knocked off her bicycle by a car on the evening of 31 July.

FATHER AND SON COVER-UP

Mr. Harvey's father, Michael, had previously confessed to the crime but later admitted that he had been covering up for his son. Ronald Harvey told police that the collision was an accident and that he did not stop because he thought he had killed Miss Watkins.

He will appear before Ashfordly Magistrates on Monday.

GUN SIEGE ENDS PEACEFULLY

Brian Rogers (left) takes his attempt to avoid paying a taxi fare a little too far.

A tense siege at an Aidensfield house on Saturday ended quietly when the gunman's mother came to the door and announced that he had fallen asleep. She then proceeded to invite police officers in for a cup of tea.

The stand-off began when Brian Rogers refused to pay a taxi driver who had taken him from Whitby to his home in Upper Mill Lane. When the driver protested, a drunken Rogers allegedly threatened him with a bottle.

MOTHER SENT FOR

The driver, who does not wish to be named, contacted Ashfordly Police and P.C. Nick Rowan was sent to investigate. But Rogers retaliated by pulling a gun on the officer before locking himself in the house.

As further officers arrived at the scene, it was decided to send for Rogers' mother, Avis, in the hope that she could persuade him to surrender. Mrs. Rogers, described by neighbours as being 'as formidable as the Berlin Wall', swiftly talked her way into the house but hopes of a swift end to the situation were dashed when moments later Rogers appeared at a window holding his mother hostage. Fears for Mrs. Rogers' safety escalated when a gunshot was heard from inside the house.

BACKUP NEEDED FOR OFFICERS

After repeated police attempts to strike up a dialogue with Rogers had failed, Sgt. Oscar Blaketon decided that officers should force their way into the house. A police dog and handler were summoned as back-up.

But just as the police were about to put an end to the three-hour siege, Mrs. Rogers calmly appeared at the door with the good news that no force was necessary.

Rogers has been charged with threatening behaviour.

Ashfordly Gazette

With which is incorporated the "Ashfordly Times and North Yorkshire Advertiser"

Registered at the General Post Office as a Newspaper | Established 1856 No. 5826. | Printed and Published by HORNE & SON. LIMITED. WHITBY | FRIDAY, SEPTEMBER 1st, 1967. | 12 Pages. | Price 3½d. | Tel. 396 (Editorial Tel. 1070)

AIDENSFIELD EDITION

MAN KILLED IN COACH SMASH

'Swerved To Avoid Sheep' — Driver

Jack Abbott pictured at the quoits match.

A coach carrying the Holinsby quoits team back from the league finals at Aidensfield veered off the road on Skipley Moor on Saturday evening and careered down a bank. One passenger was killed and two others, including the driver, were seriously injured. The dead man has been named as Jack Abbott, 44, of Holinsby.

COACH TOO FAST?

The packed coach had left the car park of the Aidensfield Arms shortly before 8 p.m. Half an hour later, as dusk descended, it ran off the road on a sharp bend and plunged down a hillside before coming to rest on a precarious perch. Passengers claimed that the coach had been going too fast approaching the bend.

The driver, 42-year-old Donald Moore, captain of the Holinsby team, was freed by emergency services after being trapped beneath the steering wheel. His wife Annie was also detained overnight at Ashfordly Hospital with rib injuries.

NO HELP FOR ABBOTT

District Nurse Maggie Bolton, who was one of the first on the scene, said: 'We managed to get Mr. and Mrs. Moore out but there was nothing we could do for Mr. Abbott. He'd simply lost too much blood and died before we could get him to hospital.'

The injured list could have been much longer. P.C. Nick Rowan's young daughter Katie was due to travel on the coach but at the last minute journeyed by car instead. P.C. Rowan, who lost his wife in January, was visibly shaken when he reached the crash site and began searching for the toddler.

His relief when told that she hadn't been aboard after all was immense.

CAUSE OF DEATH

In an attempt to ascertain the cause of the crash, police questioned the coach driver in hospital. Mr. Moore told them that he had been forced to swerve to avoid a sheep.

But one passenger said: 'Everyone knows that Jack Abbott and Annie Moore were having an affair. I swear I saw Donald look in his mirror and glimpse the two of them together just before the crash. Maybe he took his eye off the road for a fatal split second.'

(match report on page 12)

AIDENSFIELD LIFT QUOITS CUP ON DISQUALIFICATION

Alfred Ventress in action for Aidensfield, watched by referee Oscar Blaketon.

The finals of the North Riding Quoits League ended in sensational fashion at Aidensfield on Saturday when Holinsby were disqualified after defeating the home team.

Holinsby, the pre-match favourites, had beaten a spirited Aidensfield team thanks largely to an inspired performance from Bill Ashby. But while Holinsby celebrated their success, one of the vanquished Aidensfield boys — local undertaker Bernie Scripps — had a nagging feeling that he had seen Ashby somewhere before ... but not at Holinsby.

SHORT-TERM RESIDENT

With the help of fellow team member Claude Jeremiah Greengrass, Mr. Scripps discovered that Ashby was still the star player for Dale Cross, making him ineligible for Holinsby. Armed with this information, Aidensfield launched a formal protest against the result.

Holinsby captain Donald Moore claimed that Bill Ashby had lived in the village for six months and would be joining the club at the next committee meeting. But referee Oscar Blaketon ruled the player ineligible as he was not yet a member of the Holinsby club.

A jubilant Mr. Greengrass said: 'They should have held their committee meeting last week! That'll teach them to try and cheat us. It's just the sort of stunt I'd expect from Donald Moore. We've never got on.'

CRICKETERS EARN DRAW

A defiant last-over effort from Bernie Scripps helped Aidensfield to a draw in Sunday's match with visiting Strensford, writes Onlooker.

Undertaker Scripps played a dead bat to the final six deliveries to enable Aidensfield to close on 76—9 in reply to Strensford's total of 147.

Scripps, an 11th hour replacement for Claude Jeremiah Greengrass who went down with a sudden injury when he saw the Strensford pace attack warming up, held on valiantly in the face of hostile bowling. At one point in proceedings he even opened his eyes.

Earlier Harold Morley top scored for Strensford with 48, his innings including a huge six which landed in an adjoining field where a bull was grazing. The ball was immediately declared lost.

NEXT WEEK

The *Gazette*'s new popular music columnist Sandra Rafferty pays tribute to Beatles manager Brian Epstein who was found dead at the weekend.

Plus the lovely Aimi Macdonald from television's *At Last The 1948 Show* says she has no intention of following Shirley Temple into politics, and all the news from the Aidensfield Harvest Festival.

HUSBAND AND HIS LOVER ON MANSLAUGHTER CHARGES

A married father-of-two and his lover have been charged with manslaughter over the death of the man's wife.

Ashfordly Police announced last night that James Phillips and Anne Fowles have been charged in connection with the death of Sylvia Phillips whose body was found in a roadside ditch near Aidensfield last Friday.

COMINGS AND GOINGS

At first it was thought that Mrs. Phillips, who had recently left her husband to live with Mike Scott, proprietor of the Black Lion in Ashfordly, had been the victim of a hit-and-run driver. But pathology reports revealed that the cause of death was a blow to the head.

Mr. Scott informed police that Mrs. Phillips had left the Black Lion on the evening of her death to visit her family in Aidensfield. Apparently she had been upset by her family's hostility to her moving out and had told Mr. Scott that she needed time to think things over. Mr. Phillips denied his wife turned up at the family home in Moor Lane but a neighbour reported seeing her enter the house on the night in question. The witness also reported hearing a violent argument coming from the house.

Confronted with this new evidence, Mr. Phillips changed his story and confessed that his wife had come to the house and that he had killed her. He claimed that she had fallen and hit her head during an argument and, to cover up his involvement, he had dumped her body by the roadside.

NO EVIDENCE

However a forensic report was unable to find any evidence that Mr. Phillips' car had been used to transport the body.

Whilst the senior CID officers in charge of the case remained convinced that Mr. Phillips' story was plausible, Aidensfield-based P.C. Nick Rowan had doubts. His suspicions were increased when another neighbour reported hearing two women arguing shortly before Mrs. Phillips' death.

LOCAL BOBBY NOT CONVINCED

'It occurred to me,' said P.C. Rowan, 'that the only neighbour who hadn't heard a row that evening was Anne Fowles. That struck me as odd. So I decided to question her. And suddenly she broke down and confessed. It was as if a weight had been lifted off her shoulders. She said that Mrs. Phillips had returned home to find her and Mr. Phillips embracing. It seems that Mrs. Phillips had decided to leave Mike Scott and go back to her husband and family but when she saw what was going on, a major argument broke out.

(continued on page 3)

LOVE TRIANGLE

(continued from page 2)

'She said that a fight started and she pushed Mrs. Phillips to the floor. As she fell, Mrs. Phillips hit her head on the fireplace. The blow killed her. Anne Fowles then used her own car to dump the body. Mr. Phillips only confessed in an attempt to cover up for her.'

The defendants will appear at Ashfordly Magistrates' Court on Monday.

VILLAGE TALK

- Fresh from his success at the Aidensfield Harvest Festival, Bill Tate is expecting further glories with his prize leeks at the North Riding Autumn Show.

- Barmaid Gina Ward, the best reason for visiting the Aidensfield Arms, could be the next Lulu. We understand that her singing has brought her to the attention of a talent spotter working for the Scottish vocalist's recording company.

- Claude Jeremiah Greengrass is rumoured to be opening up his home to tourists as a B & B.

- Ascloseasthis: P.C. Nick Rowan and schoolteacher Jo Weston.

LATE CHEMIST

Mr. Richard Halliday, proprietor of the chemist's shop on Aidensfield Green, died on Sunday, aged 62.

'MASKED MARVEL' IN IDENTITY CRISIS

(Left to right) The real 'Masked Marvel', Pat Starr, Ken Fairbrother and Claude Jeremiah Greengrass

A row broke out this week over the true identity of wrestler 'The Masked Marvel' who played to big crowds at a show in Aidensfield on Saturday.

According to unconfirmed sources, the real 'Masked Marvel' was put out of action after being bitten by a dog owned by local gardener/handyman/captain of industry Claude Jeremiah Greengrass. It is further claimed that promoter Pat Starr, worried about losing his investment after heavily advertising the show, hired an impostor, Ken Fairbrother, to take the Marvel's place.

Mr. Fairbrother of Elm Tree Lane, Holinsby, had originally put his name down to challenge the Marvel but apparently proved so convincing as the notorious wrestler that promoter Starr wanted to keep him on.

Faced with the sack, the real Marvel allegedly forced Starr to give him his job back by threatening to expose Mr. Fairbrother as an impostor in front of the audience.

Neither party was prepared to comment on the matter.

THE WORLD ABOUT US

- The BBC replaced the old Light and Third Programmes and the Home Service with Radios 1, 2, 3 and 4.

- The Queen Mary arrived in Britain at the end of her last working cruise. She is due to spend her retirement in California.

- In Hanoi, North Vietnam rejected a United States offer of peace talks.

- A British jury returned its first majority verdict when wrestler Saleh Kassem, 'The Terrible Turk', was found guilty of handbag theft at Brighton Quarter Sessions.

WOMAN FOUND GUILTY OF STALKING P.C.

P.C. Rowan with his stalker Sandra Croft in happier times.

Twenty-nine-year-old Sandra Croft was sentenced to five years' imprisonment at York Assizes this week after admitting stalking Aidensfield Police Constable Nick Rowan and attempting to murder his girlfriend. The court heard how Croft's obsession culminated in her trying to run over schoolteacher Jo Weston.

The judge, Mr. Justice Hodgson, recommended that Croft receive psychiatric treatment.

NIGHTMARE

Afterwards P.C. Rowan expressed his relief that the case was over. 'It was a nightmare for me. It got to the stage where I was constantly looking over my shoulder in case this woman was following me. But it's my job to deal with things like that. It was worse for Jo — Miss Weston — she was just an innocent pawn in the whole business.'

The court was told that Croft developed an infatuation for P.C. Rowan after he had rescued her from her burning house at Moor Lane, Aidensfield, on 8 October. The following day he visited her in hospital and she told him that she had been drinking to forget a broken love affair when the fire started.

Croft then contacted P.C. Rowan to complain that her former boyfriend, Clive Kenway, was following her. Mr. Kenway flatly denied the accusation. The following day she reported that Mr. Kenway had stolen a gold bracelet from her house.

FOLLOWED EVERYWHERE

'She seemed to be hanging around me all the time,' said P.C. Rowan. 'I even found out from Miss Weston that Miss Croft had been to her cottage. Things were really starting to get out of hand. She even rang me at Miss Weston's cottage to demand that only I should guard her.

'Mr. Kenway denied having anything to do with the missing bracelet and told me that Miss Croft had reacted badly to the break-up. In fact he said she'd got really unpleasant about it. And then I got home to find her playing with Katie. That really spooked me.

'The next thing, she said she wanted to drop all charges relating to the bracelet. She was clearly disturbed and so I asked her to stop pestering me. I was as gentle as I could be with her.'

(continued on page 6)

P.C. STALKER

(continued from page 2)

Croft used her visit to the Police House to endeavour to frame P.C. Rowan for stealing the bracelet. She planted it in a pocket of his old police jacket where it was found by the aunt of P.C. Rowan's late wife, the popular Dr. Rowan. However since the jacket had been at the cleaners at the time of the alleged theft and had only just come back, Croft's devious plan foundered.

OFFICER IN THE FRAME

She went so far as to accuse P.C. Rowan publicly of stealing the bracelet, going to Ashfordly Police Station to demand that the Aidensfield Police House be searched. But Sgt. Oscar Blaketon stopped her in her tracks by producing the bracelet which P.C. Rowan had already handed in, following Police procedures.

She knew that P.C. Rowan and Miss Weston were seeing each other and she tried to wreck the relationship by telling Miss Weston that she and P.C. Rowan were lovers. When that too failed, she made one final desperate bid to grab attention — by attempting to run Miss Weston over.

Jo Weston: a terrifying ordeal.

LUCKY ESCAPE

Miss Weston was only saved from serious injury by the bravery and quick-thinking of P.C. Rowan and his colleague P.C. Alfred Ventress. Seeing the danger, P.C. Rowan pushed Miss Weston out of the way, putting himself in the path of the car. Meanwhile P.C. Ventress drove his car in front of Croft's, forcing her to stop.

'I suppose I should feel sorry for her,' added P.C. Rowan, 'but it's hard when she's tried to kill someone I care about.'

'HIDE' DEMOLISHED

An Aidensfield man's business lay in ruins this week after a falling-out between two bird-watchers. Claude Jeremiah Greengrass was left counting the cost of his venture into tourism when the first two guests at his new bed and breakfast establishment had a spectacular argument.

TWITCHERS

Madge and Colin Flintoff from Ripon had stayed at Mr. Greengrass's premises as part of a package deal for bird-watchers and ramblers. But when Mrs. Flintoff became disenchanted with her husband's obsession with bird-watching, she commandeered Mr. Green-grass's lorry and angrily drove over the bird hide. Fortunately for Mr. Flintoff he had vacated the hide moments earlier.

FEATHERS RUFFLED

Part of Mrs. Flintoff's anger is believed to have stemmed from her dismay at the accommodation provided by Mr. Greengrass. The couple also got hopelessly lost following the directions in Mr. Greengrass's guide. It later emerged that there was a page missing.

Last night speculation mounted that the flattened hide bore a marked similarity to the wooden scorers' hut which disappeared from Aidensfield Cricket Club two weeks ago.

The aforementioned Mr Greengrass was unavailable for comment.

A TALE OF TWO SANTAS

Children who thought there was only one Father Christmas saw their illusions shattered on Monday when two Santa Claus turned up simultaneously at Aidensfield Village Hall.

P.C. Alfred Ventress of Ashfordly Police had originally been recruited to act as Santa for Aidensfield Village School's nativity play. But when he became stuck in a snowdrift, organisers hastily employed the services of local character Claude Jeremiah Greengrass as his replacement.

VENTRESS VS GREENGRASS

Eager not to disappoint his young audience, P.C. Ventress eventually battled through the snow, only to walk into the hall at exactly the same time as Mr. Greengrass.

'There wasn't much "Ho, ho, ho" when they saw each other,' said one observer. 'I thought they were going to come to blows.'

Schoolteacher Joanna Weston explained: 'We hadn't expected P.C. Ventress to be able to make it and we didn't want the children not to have a Santa. So Mr. Greengrass stepped in. It was just one of those things that they arrived together.'

EGGS AND POO

Eight-year-old James Ashbourne was unimpressed by both Santas. He said: 'One smelled of boiled eggs, the other of farmyard poo.'

Santa One: Mr. Greengrass ...

... Santa Two: P.C. Ventress.

WHAT'S ALL THIS THEN?

Police officers hunting an escaped convict believed to be hiding out in a caravan were left with red faces on Saturday. Acting on a tip-off, they raided a caravan parked in a field near Aidensfield ... and came face to face with a pair of naturists. 'I didn't know where to put my truncheon' said one officer.

THE WORLD ABOUT US

– The world's first human recipient of a heart transplant, Cape Town grocer Louis Washkansky, continues to do well. The operation was carried out 12 days ago by Professor Barnard.

– The world's first supersonic airliner, the Anglo-French Concorde, was rolled out of its hangar in Toulouse.

– The Lawn Tennis Association voted to end the distinction between amateurs and professionals in the game.

– The Beatles had their 13th number one hit with 'Hello Goodbye'. It was revealed that their film *Magical Mystery Tour* will be shown on television on Boxing Day.

WHAT'S ON
. . . .

Saturday. Whitby Essoldo. Tony Rivers and the Castaways. 7.30pm. 9s 0d.

Saturday–Friday. Ashfordly Regal. *Blow Up.* 2.25pm, 7.30pm.

Saturday–Friday. Whitby Gaumont. *Bonnie and Clyde.* 2.30pm, 7.15pm.

Wednesday. Aidensfield Village Hall. Ashfordly Townswomen's Guild Debate: Flower Power — Who Does The Arrangements? 2pm. Coffee 7d.

PIGSTY BODY: RIDDLE SOLVED

— Wife Told 'Porkies'

The mystery surrounding the disappearance of an Aidensfield Special Constable was finally solved on Thursday when he calmly walked into Ashfordly Police Station.

For the past week speculation has been mounting that Hector Cowley had met a gruesome death, the most popular theory being that he had been fed to a local farmer's pigs. But eventually his wife Anthea admitted that she had been lying about his whereabouts. She had known all along that there was nothing sinister about his absence — he was simply away on holiday.

Here is the countdown to the saga:

DAY ONE

Special Constable Hector Cowley fails to turn up for morning traffic duty. Anthea Cowley tells P.C. Nick Rowan that she last saw her husband when he went to confront local pig farmer Betty Sutch after a load of pig manure had been dumped on his driveway. Mrs. Cowley seems unconcerned about his disappearance. P.C. Rowan visits the Sutch farm and notices that Mrs. Sutch's son Simon is wearing a Special Constable's jacket. Simon claims he bought the jacket in a second-hand shop but closer examination of the garment reveals the initials 'HC' on the inside. Simon changes his story and says that he found the jacket in the pigsty.

DAY TWO

Sgt. Oscar Blaketon of Ashfordly Police orders a search of the Sutch farm. The pig sty throws up further items of uniform. Mrs. Sutch tells the police that next to the sty she found a wheelbarrow which did not belong to her. She comes up with a solid alibi for the night of Mr. Cowley's disappearance — a secret lover who spent the night with her. Rumours *(continued on page 6)*

(continued on page 6)

PIGSTY PUZZLE

(continued from page 5)

begin to circulate around the village that Hector Cowley has been eaten by pigs.

DAY THREE

P.C. Rowan informs Mrs. Cowley that her husband's uniform has been found in the pigsty at the Sutch farm. At the Cowley house, P.C. Rowan notices a bundle of men's clothing burning in a garden incinerator. Mrs. Cowley admits that she had an argument with her husband but denies any knowledge of his whereabouts.

DAY FOUR

P.C. Rowan and Sgt. Blaketon tackle Mrs. Cowley about the wheelbarrow. She confesses that it belongs to her husband and that she used it to dump his beloved police uniform in the Sutches' pigsty. She explains that they had a bitter argument because she refused to go on holiday with Mr. Cowley's sister and brother-in-law. After Mr. Cowley had gone away on his own, Mrs. Cowley neglected to post a letter informing Ashfordly Police that he was taking a holiday.

DAY EIGHT

Hector Cowley returns from holiday, oblivious to the drama. Sgt. Blaketon was not amused by the goings-on. 'Mrs. Cowley's deliberate failure to forward her husband's letter to me and subsequent refusal to divulge the fact that he was on holiday has resulted in the wasting of a great deal of police time. She may yet find herself facing charges.'

BOY RESCUED

P.C. Nick Rowan with the runaway, Dennis Cross.

Ten-year-old Dennis Cross of Holme Cottage, Aidensfield, was rescued by P.C. Nick Rowan on Tuesday after falling down a gully and knocking himself out. The boy, who had run away from home, was being pursued by P.C. Rowan when he plunged into the abyss in a field off Moor Lane. He was taken to Ashfordly Hospital where he was treated for mild concussion.

NIGHT-WATCHMAN FAKED ROBBERY

Elderly night-watchman Albert Potter invented a robbery in an attempt to prove to his boss that he was still useful, Ashfordly Magistrates heard.

On 21 December Potter, night-watchman at Sangers factory, phoned the police to report that he had been attacked by masked raiders. He said that the men knocked him down and escaped with some petty cash but were scared off when he told them that he had called the police. For that reason, he added, the wages in the safe were untouched.

However when a man was arrested in connection with the raid, Potter admitted that he made the whole thing up to show that he was worth keeping on. He was put on probation for two years.

LOCAL MAN TRICKED BY AUSTRALIAN COUPLE

Local businessman Claude Jeremiah Greengrass has been left licking his wounds after apparently being conned out of an antique desk by a young Australian couple. Although Mr. Greengrass has elected not to press charges, Ashfordly Police have built up a precise picture of the unfortunate sequence of events.

WEALTHY COUPLE

Sgt. Oscar Blaketon told the *Gazette*: 'We understand that Mr. Greengrass met an Australian couple, Len and Julie Wilcox, who were searching for ancestral gravestones. When he learned that they were wealthy, he thought that there might be something in it for him.

'So, in his usual helpful manner, he showed them round all the local graveyards until they had found the gravestones they were looking for. Then he claimed that he was distantly related to them.

'It seems that his intention was to try and persuade Mr. Wilcox to buy some property in the area and to let him (Greengrass) manage it for them. After all, if you can't trust your own flesh and blood, who can you trust?

'Whether they swallowed this story about him being related to them we don't know, but they certainly didn't take him up on his business offer. So Mr. Greengrass tried a new tack and told them he was related to aristocracy. Furthermore he was willing to sell certain family heirlooms to them.

'ANTIQUE' SALE

'Certain that he had found a pair of suckers who would pay way over the odds for anything, he went and bought a number of antiques which he planned to pass off as these 'family heirlooms' and sell to the Wilcoxes.

'But it would appear that they had seen him coming. For no sooner had he handed over an antique desk — purportedly belonging to Lady Hermione Greengrass, no doubt — than our friends from Down Under had skipped Aidensfield without paying him for it. All in all, I would say it was a classic case of the biter bit.'

Claude Jeremiah Greengrass — will not be pressing charges.

TEACHER'S MOTHER DIES

Mrs. Fiona Weston of Rook Cottage, Aidensfield, died in Ashfordly Hospital on Wednesday from a suspected cerebral haemorrhage. She was 52. She leaves behind a husband Graham and daughter Jo, a schoolteacher at Aidensfield Village School. The funeral will be at Aidensfield Church on Monday.

DOG SNATCHED IN BUN ROW

A hot cross bun man. Cliff Dyson with local barmaid Gina Ward.

A family feud erupted this week over the recipe for the famous Aidensfield Buns. As matters threatened to get out of hand, a local man's dog was kidnapped as a possible ransom for the recipe.

FAVOURITES

Aidensfield Buns have been a favourite with locals and tourists alike for the past 30 years. Their recipe has always been closely guarded to ward off imitations but in recent months they have vanished from the shelves following the confinement of their creator, baker Bill Dyson, to a nursing home. To the dismay of his sons, Cliff and Frank (who were frequently at loggerheads), Mr. Dyson flatly refused to divulge the secret recipe to them.

However last Friday Mr. Dyson at last decided to reveal the recipe to someone he thought he could trust — local man Claude Jeremiah Greengrass. Mr. Dyson wrote down the recipe and gave it to Mr. Greengrass for safekeeping, saying that he was worried that his warring sons would destroy the business through their refusal to work together.

RECIPE SALE

According to the Dyson brothers, Mr. Greengrass tried to auction off the recipe to the highest bidder. Cliff Dyson told the *Gazette*: 'He told me and Frank separately that he had the bun recipe and to prove it he had a batch made. He was trying to play us off against each other — to sell it to whoever would pay most.

BUNS HOT UP

'Things got a bit heated between Frank and me and we realised that was playing into Greengrass's hands. So we buried the hatchet and kidnapped his dog, Alfred. We knew he thought the world of that mutt and would hand over the recipe rather than risk any harm coming to the dog. Not that we would have done anything like that, you understand. We just wanted what was rightfully ours.'

(continued on page 9)

BUN FIGHT

(continued from page 8)

'We didn't see why some money-grabbing outsider should profit from the Aidensfield Buns. Why should Greengrass have his cake and eat it?'

Negotiations between the two parties proved a tense affair but eventually Mr. Greengrass backed down and agreed to hand over the recipe in return for Alfred. Sgt. Oscar Blaketon of Ashfordly Police supervised the exchange on Wednesday.

On the orders of Mr. Dyson, the recipe was given to both sons...even though it was no longer a secret.

Cliff Dyson promised yesterday: 'It won't be long before Aidensfield Buns are back in the shops.'

Mr. Greengrass strongly denied that he already had a batch awaiting delivery.

FIRM 'BACKING BRITAIN'

A dozen female employees at Heathfield Pickles of Aidensfield have joined the 'I'm Backing Britain' campaign. The girls have promised to work an extra half-hour every day, without pay.

The campaign, launched by five typists at a factory in Surbiton, Surrey, last month, aims to put the 'Great' back into Great Britain. It has won nationwide support and the backing of the government. Doing his bit for the cause, entertainer Bruce Forsyth has released a record called 'I'm Backing Britain'.

FRUIT & VEG man required
Must be experienced
TEL: ASH 230

The police are on hand in case trouble breaks out at the recipe handover.

WINTER SPECIAL OFFER
Golden Frome Tea
(the tea for the connoisseur)
was 1s 9d NOW 1s 6d

County Stores, Chapel Row, Ashfordly

LANDLORD RETIRES

George Ward, landlord of the Aidensfield Arms, announced this week that he is having to retire from the licensing trade because of ill health.

'I've had nearly 20 years at the Aidensfield Arms,' said Mr. Ward, 'and I've enjoyed practically every minute —apart from the odd set-to at closing time. But I'm not as young as I used to be and I get tired quickly. I can't be done with humping barrels.

'It will be a wrench because I've made a lot of friends in the village and I'll miss them all. But it's time to put my feet up.'

Mr. Ward's comely niece Gina, an asset to any establishment, plans to stay on at the hostelry.

THE WORLD ABOUT US

- Escaped Great Train Robber Charles Wilson was arrested in Canada.

- The National Provincial Bank and the Westminster Bank announced that they are to merge.

- Former American vice-president Richard Nixon said that he will run for president.

- The island of Mauritius gained independence from Britain.

Ashfordly Gazette

With which is incorporated the "Ashfordly Times and North Yorkshire Advertiser"

Registered at the General Post Office as a Newspaper   Established 1856 No. 5859.   Printed and Published by HORNE & SON, LIMITED, WHITBY   FRIDAY, APRIL 12th, 1968.   12 Pages.   Price 3½d.   Tel. 396 (Editorial Tel. 1070)

AIDENSFIELD EDITION

DARING TRAIN ROBBERY FOILED

– Police Arrest Fur Gang

Police officers swooped on a train moments after it had left Aidensfield Station on Tuesday and arrested a gang who had targeted a consignment of fur coats that was on board. Two men were arrested on the spot and a third was picked up yesterday.

With echoes of the Great Train Robbery, the gang had tampered with signals to bring the train to a halt a mile south of Aidensfield. The robbers quickly located the fur coats but before they could make their escape via a waiting car, police officers, who had been watching one of the gang for several days, arrived in force.

DRAMATIC CHASE BY P.C.s

One gang member forced the driver to start up the train but P.C. Nick Rowan and P.C. Phil Bellamy managed to jump aboard. Chasing the robbers through the carriages, they eventually apprehended two men. The third —

Ainsworth, recently released from prison, will soon be back behind bars.

Ainswoth's wife Molly betrayed her employers at the fur factory.

Eddie Ainsworth, a known villain — leapt from the moving train but was captured in a woodland hideaway two days later.

Officers had been keeping an eye on Ainsworth, who had recently been released from prison after serving a sentence for armed robbery, from the moment he turned up in Aidensfield last week.

INVESTIGATION

Sgt. Oscar Blaketon of Ashfordly Police revealed: 'We had been investigating a number of missing fur offcuts from De Vere's factory where Ainsworth's wife Molly worked. We knew she was behind with the rent and, giv-

en the family background, thought she might know something about the disappearing furs.

LIKE FATHER, LIKE SON

'Meanwhile P.C. Rowan had cause to reprimand the Ainsworths' 11-year-old son Terry for travelling on a train without a ticket. It was on a visit to the house that he discovered that Eddie Ainsworth was out of jail. Eddie seemed to be spending a lot of time with his son and showing a sudden interest in the boy's passion for trains. We know that they took at least one train journey together.

(continued on page 6)

TRAIN ROBBERY

Young Terry Ainsworth (left) was looking after his father in Aidensfield Wood.

(continued from page 1)

'We heard about a pair of mink earrings bought from Ashfordly Market and traced the trader who was selling the fur off-cuts. The manager at De Vere's, Mr. Jenkins, confirmed that a mink cravat retrieved from the market had earlier been stolen from the factory.

FACTORY THEFT

'We quizzed Mrs. Ainsworth about the thefts but one of her colleagues confessed that she had stolen the pelt so that she could lend Mrs. Ainsworth the rent money. The woman also happened to mention that Eddie Ainsworth had been questioning his wife about transport arrangement for a batch of fur coats. That, plus the fact that a couple of trespassers had been spotted acting suspiciously on the railway line the day before, set alarm bells ringing.'

Mr. Jenkins told the police that the train carrying the fur coats had just left Aidensfield Station and so they set off in hot pursuit.

TRAIL TO FOLLOW

'It was a highly successful operation,' continued Sgt. Blaketon, 'apart from the fact that Ainsworth got away. We knew he hadn't gone far but Mrs. Ainsworth was refusing to co-operate. Then P.C. Rowan spotted young Terry carrying a rucksack full of food and persuaded the boy to lead us to his father. It seems that Terry was disappointed that his father had used him to plan the robbery. He felt a bit betrayed. And so he led us to his secret den in Aidensfield Wood where Eddie was lying low.'

Ainsworth was arrested without a struggle and was later charged with armed robbery. He will appear in court next week.

WATER TORTURE

– 'Community Service' goes wrong

An Aidensfield man's hunt for valuable Roman coins ended in disaster when he cracked a water main and caused hundreds of pounds of damage to a family's garden. Local handyman Claude Jeremiah Greengrass was clearing undergrowth from the bottom of a garden in Upper Mill Lane when houseowner Mrs. Dobson informed him that she had lost her diamond ring somewhere in the vicinity.

GENEROUS ACT

'Trying to be helpful and find her ring for her, I went to the expense of hiring a metal detector,' said Mr. Greengrass who denied that his actions were driven by the prospect of a reward. 'I couldn't find no ring but I did unearth a Roman coin.

'The Dobsons were away for a few days so it occurred to me that there might be more Roman coins buried in the garden. If I found

Claude Jeremiah Greengrass, once more on the trail of lost treasure.

any I was going to hand them over to some museum. There was definitely nothing in it for me. The gratitude of my nation would have been sufficient.

TALE OF WOE

'I got a strong signal from the middle of the lawn so I was sure I was on to something, but it's heavy work digging so I thought I could speed things up by borrowing one of them mechanical diggers. I got my mate Bernie Scripps to lend me one and off I went. I was doing fine till all this water started gushing out. What a daft place to put a water main — under ground where no one can see it.'

North Riding Water Board were called out to deal with the fractured main and, to add insult to injury, the workmen discovered a pot of Roman coins which they promptly handed over to the Dobsons.

Asked about the scene of devastation which they had returned home to, Mr. Dobson said: 'Suffice to say that Mr. Greengrass will not be doing any more gardening jobs for us.'

Bernie Scripps ... provided the mechanical digger.

THE WORLD ABOUT US

– Riots flared in America following the assassination of Civil Rights leader Dr. Martin Luther King in Memphis.

– Pierre Trudeau became Prime Minister of Canada.

– Former world motor racing champion Jim Clark was killed in a crash at Hockenheim, West Germany.

– Spain's 'La La La' pipped the United Kingdom's 'Congratulations', sung by Cliff Richard, to win the Eurovision Song Contest.

THE BUTLER DID IT!

— Con Man Guilty Of Moor Shooting

P.C. Nick Rowan (right) with Barry Rooksby.

A man who posed as a butler to steal from an elderly widow has been convicted of theft and of attempting to murder a former workmate. Reginald Dale was sentenced to seven years' imprisonment at York Assizes by Judge Carver who described him as 'an unscrupulous and highly dangerous individual.'

On 3 November last, the police received an anonymous phone call giving the location of an injured man on Kirlby Moor. There they found a man suffering from gunshot wounds. He was subsequently identified as Sammy Maxton, gamekeeper at Puckton Hall near Strensford.

RUNNING SCARED

A car seen parked in the area at the time of the shooting was identified as belonging to Barry Rooksby, Mr. Maxton's predecessor as gamekeeper. Mr. Rooksby told officers that he had witnessed the shooting from a distance. It was he who had made the anonymous call to the police.

He told the court that he had driven off in a hurry because he was frightened of being implicated.

Jonathan Partington, QC, prosecuting described how, in the course of his inquiries, P.C. Nick Rowan had gone to Puckton Hall to interview Dale, the odd-job man. However Dale had suddenly disappeared, along with an antique pool table belonging to the owner of Puckton Hall, Colonel Hepworth.

MORE MISSING ITEMS

The pool table was traced to local man Claude Jeremiah Greengrass who said that he had purchased it legitimately from a dealer, Cyril Fetter. Mr. Fetter told the police that one of the men who had sold him the table was Sammy Maxton.

Meanwhile a number of items had mysteriously disappeared from the Aidensfield home of elderly widow Alice Jessop. She had recently taken on a butler/housekeeper by the

name of Lester who had answered her advertisement in the *Gazette*.

Returning from a hospital check-up, Mrs. Jessop and District Nurse Maggie Bolton saw the man calling himself Lester driving away from the house. Inside they found that the place had been burgled.

(continued on page 11)

BUTLER CASE

(continued from page 5)

Medical tests showed that 'Lester' had been spiking Mrs. Jessop's medication with alcohol.

P.C. Rowan and P.C. Phil Bellamy followed 'Lester''s car to Mr. Fetter's shop where they apprehended him and unmasked him as Dale. He turned out to be a habitual con man wanted for a series of similar offences.

SHOOTING

When Sammy Maxton recovered from his wounds, he pointed the finger at Dale for the shooting. Mr. Maxton testified: 'I found out that Dale was stealing from Puckton Hall and said I wanted in on it in return for keeping quiet. Dale promised me a cut and arranged to meet me up on the moor. Instead he shot me in cold blood.'

Defending, Ivor Smedley, QC, said that his client deeply regretted his actions and was intending to put his life of deception behind him. To that end, he had purchased a second-hand car business.

P.C. WEDS TEACHER

The happy couple with P.C. Rowan's child from his previous marriage.

The newlyweds climb aboard on the first stage of their honeymoon.

Village Police Constable Nick Rowan and local schoolteacher Jo Weston were married at Aidensfield Church, on Saturday. The happy couple set off on honeymoon to an undisclosed destination.

The day was momentarily marred by an unseemly scuffle at the wedding reception when local man Claude Jeremiah Greengrass and the groom's grandfather came to blows over the disputed ownership of some jellied eels. Both were ejected by Sgt. Oscar Blaketon of Ashfordly Police.

NEW LICENSEE

Gina Ward, niece of retired landlord George Ward, has succeeded him as licensee of the Aidensfield Arms. The fair Gina, who last year sang as warm-up at a local wrestling show, says she may install a jukebox with all the up-to-date sounds.

THE WORLD ABOUT US

- Britain introduced its first decimal coins — the five New Pence coin, which will eventually replace the shilling, and the ten New Pence coin which will succeed the two-shilling piece.

- Conservative MP Enoch Powell triggered a fierce race row by predicting a 'river of blood' if immigration is allowed to continue at its present rate.

- At the age of 69, Louis Armstrong topped the British hit parade for the first time with 'What a Wonderful World'.

Ashfordly Gazette

With which is incorporated the "Ashfordly Times and North Yorkshire Advertiser"

Registered at the General Post Office as a Newspaper · Established 1856 No. 5862. · Printed and Published by HORNE & SON. LIMITED. WHITBY · FRIDAY, MAY 3rd, 1968. · 12 Pages. · Price 3'/.d. · Tel. 396 (Editorial Tel. 1070)

AIDENSFIELD EDITION

MAN SHOT IN 'BONNIE AND CLYDE'-STYLE WAGES SNATCH

— Police Sergeant Suffers Heart Attack

A construction site manager was shot in the shoulder and a police sergeant suffered a heart attack in the course of a violent payroll robbery at Boisdale Moor on Tuesday lunchtime. The two armed robbers — a man and a woman in their late twenties — were apprehended when their getaway car crashed and burst into flames.

GREENGRASS AND WARD

Also caught up in the day's dramatic events were local speculator Claude Jeremiah Greengrass and Gina Ward, the shapely new licensee of the Aidensfield Arms. Both were held at gunpoint during the raid and were left in no doubt that they would be shot if they made one false move.

The robbery took place at a pipeline compound high up on the moor. The 100-strong workforce had demanded that their outstanding wages be paid direct to the site within 24 hours or they would down tools. Consequently £6,140 was to be delivered by

Sharma Semple: robbery charges.

security van. Clearly the robbers knew about the abnormally large sum on board.

ENTREPRENEURS UNITE

Mr. Greengrass had been doing a daily sandwich run to the site, selling produce from the Aidensfield Arms. The remoteness of the compound meant that he had plenty of customers. But Miss Ward felt that the financial returns were not matching the sales (continued on page 2)

WAGES SNATCH

(continued from page 1)

and so on Monday she told her business partner that she would be joining him on the following day's run.

'I tried to talk her out of it,' said Mr. Greengrass yesterday. 'I told her how rough it could be up there but she wouldn't listen. She seemed to have got it into her head that I was diddling her. I can't think where she got an idea like that. I bet she wishes she'd listened to old Claude now.'

HIPPIES

Mr. Greengrass' truck, with Miss Ward and a pile of sandwiches as passengers, set out from Aidensfield shortly after 10am. Twenty minutes into their journey, they saw a couple standing by the side of the road. They recognised them as a pair of hippies who had been in the Aidensfield Arms the previous evening. The man said that their car had overheated and asked for a lift. When Mr. Greengrass appeared reluctant, the man pulled a gun on him. The hippie outfits were their disguises.

After reversing their own car into woods, the robbers forced Mr. Greengrass to follow the Ravelin Security van to the compound.

'They jumped into the back of Claude's truck and smashed the rear window,' said Miss Ward. 'There was glass everywhere. And then the man pointed a shotgun at us through the broken window just to make sure we did as we were told.'

When the truck reached the compound, the robbers hid under a tarpaulin in the back while the security guard delivered the wages to the site office. The site manager, Ronald Corbett, then put the money into the safe.

VIOLENCE

Once the security van had driven off, the robbers pounced. Still holding Mr. Greengrass and Miss Ward at gunpoint, they burst into the

P.C. Mike Bradley tends the wounded Alfred.

site office. Mr. Corbett was hit a savage blow on the side of the head with the butt of the shotgun and told to open the safe. When Mr. Corbett hesitated, the man went out and shot Mr. Greengrass' dog Alfred. He warned that Mr. Greengrass and Miss Ward would be next. Mr. Corbett had no choice but to open the safe.

OFFICERS ARRIVE

Just as they were about to make their escape, the robbers heard the sound of an approaching motorcycle. Aware of the payroll delivery, Sgt. Oscar Blaketon had ordered his officers to make regular trips up to the site office. This one was being made by P.C. Mike Bradley on only his second day at Ashfordly after being transferred up from London.

(continued on page 6)

ARMED ROBBERY

(continued from page 2)

Loading the cash bags into the truck, the male robber jumped into the back and trained his shotgun on Mr. Greengrass and Miss Ward. He told them to act naturally. Meanwhile the woman hid behind a door in the site office, aiming a revolver at Mr. Corbett.

AGGRESSION

'She told me to get rid of the police officer,' said Mr. Corbett. 'And she warned me that she was a better shot than her accomplice whom she called Terry. From the tone of her voice and the look in her eyes, I believed her.'

'Straight away I could sense something wasn't quite right,' said P.C. Bradley. 'I chatted to Mr. Greengrass and Miss Ward, both of whom I had met the previous evening, but they were curiously silent, uptight.

'I then went into the site office to see Mr. Corbett. He was sitting at his desk with his arms folded but he was pointing his finger towards the empty safe. I was now certain that something was up. I stood on the steps of the office and looked out over the compound. I was trying to appear calm but there was an eerie feeling. Then I saw a movement from beside a pile of pallets. It was Mr. Greengrass' dog. There were specks of

blood on his hind leg.'

Worried that she could no longer see P.C. Bradley, the female robber emerged from her hiding place. Mr. Corbett seized the opportunity and tried to overpower her. But as he crept towards her, a floorboard creaked and she turned round and shot him in the shoulder.

Hearing the gunshot, P.C. Bradley broke cover and sprinted towards the site office, only to be felled by a blow from the shotgun butt wielded by the male robber. He recovered consciousness in time to see the truck disappearing down the hill.

NO WAY TO FOLLOW

The raiders had immobilised the police motorcycle and cut down the telephone lines but P.C. Bradley managed to repair his motorcycle radio and inform P.C. Alfred Ventress at Ashfordly Station about the robbery. A mile from the compound, the robbers switched to their hidden Rover, leaving Mr. Greengrass and Miss Ward shaken but unharmed. They were able to give the police a description of the getaway car.

The Rover headed east on the B151 and then south towards Pickering on the B169 with several police vehicles and Mr. Greengrass' truck in hot pursuit.

(continued on page 7)

P.C. Mike Bradley pictured before his visit to the barber's.

ROBBERY DRAMA

Sgt. Blaketon, shortly before his heart attack.

(continued from page 6)

Mr. Greengrass's knowledge of short-cuts enabled him to catch the Rover and from the opposite direction on a blind hill came Sgt. Blaketon. Seeing the police car too late, the Rover swerved off the road and into a huge boulder.

OFFICER DOWN

Sgt. Blaketon disarmed the man with a blow from his truncheon and tried to pull the unconscious woman from the burning car. But her weight proved too much for him and he sank to his knees, clutching his chest. Mr. Greengrass bravely dragged both Sgt. Blaketon and the female robber clear of the car, seconds before it exploded. The male robber made a last attempt to escape but was halted in his tracks by Miss Ward pointing the shotgun.

Emergency crews were quickly on the scene and the wounded were rushed to Ashfordly Hospital where Sgt. Blaketon was diagnosed as having suffered a heart attack. Last night he was said to be satisfactory.

A hospital spokesman said: 'He told us that his biggest shock was waking up in the ambulance and seeing Mr. Greengrass next to him. And when he heard that it was Mr. Greengrass who had saved his life, he nearly had another heart attack!'

WANTED

Police have charged Terry and Sharma Semple with armed robbery. It is understood that Terry Semple is already wanted for questioning about a number of similar wages snatches in the south, including one in which a security guard was murdered.

POLICE SERGEANT TO RETIRE

Who's smiling now? Mr. Blaketon relaxing.

Sgt. Oscar Blaketon of Ashfordly Police has had to take early retirement from the force through ill health. Sgt. Blaketon, who has been an officer for 22 years, suffered a heart attack just over three weeks ago and, although he has recovered, has been ruled unfit to resume duty.

SHOCKER

'It was a bit of a shock at first,' admitted Sgt. Blaketon this week, 'but now I've got used to it, I'm looking forward to a new career running Aidensfield Post Office. And any villains can rest assured that even though I'm no longer in uniform, I'll still be keeping my eyes open.'

Among those who paid tribute to Sgt. Blaketon was his old adversary, Claude Jeremiah Greengrass. 'I know me and Sgt. Blaketon had our differences — he's shorter than me for a start — but in a funny way I'll miss him, rather like Jerry would miss Tom.'

P.C. LOCKED IN HORSEBOX

Police Constable Alfred Ventress of Ashfordly Police spent an uncomfortable 14 hours locked in a horsebox after being kidnapped by horse thieves. He eventually managed to untie his bonds and escaped by driving the horsebox away. The Deightons, a well-known family of travelling tinkers, were last night being questioned by police in connection with the incident.

It is believed that P.C. Ventress was taken captive after trying to foil an attempt at switching two racehorses. As a widespread search was launched to trace the missing officer, P.C. Ventress was tied up in the box with only an equine friend for company.

ODOROUS

P.C. Phil Bellamy said of his colleague's ordeal: 'The smell must have been awful. I don't know how the horse put up with it.'

THE WORLD ABOUT US

– A gas explosion has been blamed for the collapse of part of the 22-storey East London tower block, Ronan Point, in which three people died.

– Student protesters and striking trade unionists brought France to a standstill.

– West Bromwich Albion beat Manchester City 1–0 in the FA Cup final.

'HAUNTED HOUSE' FORCED TO CLOSE

An Aidensfield house which the owner claimed to be haunted was closed to tourists this week on the orders of the Paranormal Research Institute. Claude Jeremiah Greengrass had earlier told investigators from the institute that his land was haunted by three separate ghosts — those of Lady Ashfordly (the White Lady), a headless horseman and a mysterious dog known as the 'Ashfordly Hound'.

SPOOKY

Having witnessed for themselves the manifestation of the hound in the form of a glowing creature striding across Mr. Greengrass' top field at night, the investigators were suitably impressed. 24 hours later he opened his premises to the public and did a thriving trade charging a shilling a head to view the various apparitions.

CROOKED

But investigators took a dim view on discovering that the 'Ashfordly Hound' was nothing more than Mr. Greengrass' own dog, Alfred, wearing an old sack coated in luminous paint.

The day after the news broke there were more long queues outside Mr. Greengrass' home — this time disgruntled sightseers demanding their money back.

Schoolteacher and Policeman bid tearful goodbyes to friends from Aidensfield before leaving for Canada.

FOND FAREWELL

Aidensfield said farewell this week to its popular village bobby, P.C. Nick Rowan, who is emigrating to Canada with his schoolteacher wife Jo. P.C. Rowan, who has served the village for four years, is taking up a post with the Canadian Police, in Canada.

At their farewell party at the Aidensfield Arms, the couple were presented with a goat.

Twenty-five-year-old P.C. Mike Bradley will be the new occupant of the Aidensfield Police House. Like his predecessor, he served with the Metropolitan Police in London before moving up to the more civilised area of Yorkshire.

POST OFFICE RAID NETS £800

— Elderly Woman Knocked Over By Fleeing Robber

A young robber snatched a mail bag containing over £800 in a daring raid at Aidensfield Post Office yesterday morning. As the robber fled to a waiting getaway car, he knocked over 80-year-old Sarah Thorpe. She was taken to hospital but not detained overnight.

MISSING PENSION

The robbery happened at 8.30am as postman Fred Pearson delivered the week's pension money. Hearing the sound of a window being smashed on the Post Office van, postmaster Oscar Blaketon, himself recently retired from the police force, rushed to investigate. The robber, who had been waiting in the shop pretending to choose a newspaper, snatched one of the bags from the Mr. Blaketon and headed for the back door. On his way out, he barged into Mrs. Thorpe.

The getaway car, driven by a female accomplice, was waiting in an alley alongside the Post Office. It is thought that the female robber had been responsible for breaking the window of the van — a ruse designed to distract Mr. Blaketon. A half-brick was found at the scene.

GREENGRASS' GUESTS

The robbers — both in their early twenties — are thought to have stayed in a room at Claude Jeremiah Greengrass' house on the night before the raid. 'They even left without having breakfast,' said Mr. Greengrass. 'And it was all included in the very reasonable price.'

Acting on information from Mr. Greengrass that the woman was called Mitzi, police named the suspects as Mitzi and Johnny Wyler. She is the daughter of Jimmy Turpin who had been seen in Aidensfield earlier in the week following his release from prison. Turpin had once been put away by Oscar Blaketon and one theory is that Turpin masterminded the robbery as some form of belated revenge.

INSIDE JOB

Police also believe the robbers had some sort of inside information since they knew which of the two bags to snatch. The contents of the bag not taken was worthless.

THE WORLD ABOUT US

– Russian tanks closed in on Czechoslovakia.

– In an encyclical entitled 'Humanae Vitae' (Of Human Life), Pope Paul declared the Catholic Church's opposition to all forms of birth control.

– Palestinian Arab immigrant Sirhan Sirhan pleaded not guilty to the murder of Senator Robert Kennedy, shot dead in Los Angeles on 5 June.

– Controversy surrounded the start of a new BBC comedy series, *Dad's Army*, which pokes fun at Britain's war effort. The show is not expected to last more than one series.

THE STORY OF HEARTBEAT

<u>Presenting another in our series of special colour supplements about the stars of the hit television programme *Heartbeat* which is filmed in our region.</u>

WILLIAM SIMONS as P.C. ALF VENTRESS

'The day Ventress joined the police he was looking forward to retirement,' smiles William Simons. 'To be honest he's a bit of a failure. The only thing he's good at is not doing much — and he's got that down to a fine art. For ages he had never been seen driving on the show so when we finally had him drive, we decided he'd be a bad driver. That sums him up.

'The rural setting suits him because the work is more leisurely and he knows what he can get away with. He's more wary of Craddock whereas he'd been with Blaketon so long he knew him. He is by no means untypical however. I met a Ventress quite recently while we were out filming. This policeman noticed that I was smoking on duty while walking down the street and said to me: "I wish I could get away with that."

'He manages to store information — he's like a smoking filing-cabinet. In fact with all the hard-boiled eggs he eats, he's a smelly, smoking filing-cabinet. And yes I do have to eat all those eggs — I do all my own stunts!

'The smoking would have been more of a problem. I remember when I was offered the part, it was described as a chain-smoking policeman. But I'm not a smoker so I smoke herbal cigarettes on the show. I was actually away in France when casting was taking place but I came back and got the part. So it was a worthwhile journey.'

William is no stranger to police roles. In 1981 he starred as Detective Constable Thackeray in the Victorian detective series *Cribb* and has played policemen in, among others, *Bergerac*, *The Bill* and *Inspector Alleyn*. 'For the first two and a half years of *Heartbeat* I played Ventress and Inspector Fox in *Alleyn* back to back. At one point they even went out on opposing channels on the same night. Over the years I've gone up and down the ranks, from Chief Superintendent to humble Constable. All in all, I've played so many cops I think I'll probably be buried in blue!'

MARK JORDON as P.C. PHIL BELLAMY

M ark Jordon might have ended up becoming a policeman instead of playing one ... but he deliberately failed the entrance exam.

Mark explains: 'My mum used to be the civilian secretary at Oldham Police Station and would often take me along when I was young. At 17 I applied to join the Police Cadets — really just to please my mum — but I didn't fancy it so I deliberately failed. By then I had already decided that I wanted to act and had several irons in the fire but I must admit I was frightened in case the police accepted me.'

But the experience gleaned from studying the police at close quarters has not been wasted in Mark's acting career. 'I was P.C. Betts in *Coronation Street* who helped investigate the disappearance of Tracy Barlow. I also played P.C. Hicks in an episode of *All Creatures Great and Small* — where I had to arrest Peter Benson who plays Bernie Scripps in *Heartbeat* — and I was a young D.I. in *Shoot To Kill*. But it's as Bellamy that I've been able to put most of my early learning to good use. I remember at Oldham that they never took the sergeant seriously, how quiet it was most of the time and how the officers got so bored that they'd play jokes on each other. I've been able to apply that to *Heartbeat*. Bellamy is the station joker, forever setting Alf up.

'I think of Bellamy as a YTS Jack the Lad. He thinks he's more mature than he is when really he is quite naïve. He is a complete innocent who tries too hard. He is sporty and good-natured but although basically he joined the force to improve his sex life, he never gets the girl. He's been after Gina for ages but she thinks he's a pillock. But he's fun to play, particularly because he makes so many mistakes.'

Thirty-four-year-old Mark has been married for two years to actress Siobhan Finneran and they have a year-old son, Joseph. 'We live on Saddleworth Moor which is like a Lancashire version of Goathland. The one thing I've never conquered about filming in North Yorkshire is the cold. It cuts through me and I'm always the first one to put my hand up and say it's freezing. I end up having to wear two or three layers of thermals under my uniform. I guess I'm still a townie.'

PHILIP FRANKS as SGT. RAYMOND CRADDOCK

Nobody was more amazed than Philip Franks when he was asked to play the disciplinarian Sgt. Craddock in *Heartbeat*. Philip says: 'He's Welsh, I'm not; he's tough, I'm not. And I had never played a policeman before. In fact I usually play nice people like Charlie in *The Darling Buds Of May* so I must thank producer Gerry Mill for seeing the nasty side to me!

'I was directing a play at the time and after the audition for Craddock I thought nothing will come of it and I can get back to my play. But to my surprise and delight I was offered the part.

'I made use of a Welsh friend to teach me the accent and I set about working out Craddock's look. There is a definite seam of vanity in him and because he is so meticulous, I knew that he would have nothing out of place. So I made him sleek, almost shiny and — of course — spotless. For Craddock wouldn't dream of getting dirty — he'd get Ventress to lie down in a puddle and walk over him.

'Craddock has an extremely high opinion of himself. He thinks he's an excellent policeman — fair, strict and ironic — whereas to others he is a sarcastic old martinet. He sees Aidensfield as a stepping stone towards a glittering career. He doesn't join in or socialise — the only time he goes into the pub is to arrest people. I think it's appropriate that his hobby is ballroom dancing because that requires discipline and a certain stiffness. He is not a spontaneous person. He could perhaps have been a bank manager but he would have been too vicious. For if Blaketon was a wooden club, Craddock is a rod of iron.'

Forty-year-old Philip began acting at Oxford University from where he graduated in 1978. After early work on the London fringe, he spent several seasons with the Royal Shakespeare Company and

went to New York with the 1983 RSC production of 'All's Well That Ends Well'.

His TV credits include *Bleak House*, Patsy's father in *Absolutely Fabulous* and Tom Pinch in *Martin Chuzzlewit*. He is also an accomplished director and has appeared regularly on *Countdown* and *Call My Bluff*.

TRICIA PENROSE as GINA WARD

While Tricia Penrose is pulling pints behind the bar of the Aidensfield Arms, she is secretly dreaming of appearing in a West End musical. 'I'd love to get into musicals,' says Tricia. 'I've been singing all my life. My mum and I used to sing as a duo called Second Image around the pubs and clubs of my native Merseyside and later I was part of another duo called Impulse. I've sung a few times on *Heartbeat* and in 1996 I released a version of the old Supremes' number "Where Did Our Love Go?" which I'd sung on the show. I've sung on *Vanessa*, GMTV and *Night Fever* but I suppose my ultimate ambition is to be on *Top of the Pops*.'

Tricia started acting in school plays. 'At ten I was the Wicked Witch of the West in a school production of "The Wizard of Oz". I auditioned for Dorothy but didn't get it. Anyway people told my mum and dad to put me into drama school and luckily they took the hint.

'My first TV was at the age of 14 in *Brookside*. I played Damon Grant's girlfriend Ruth. Five years later in 1989 I was back in *Brookside* as W.P.C. Emma Reid who had a fling with Rod Corkhill. I also did seven episodes of *Emmerdale* as a character called Louise who led Elsa Bates astray.'

Tricia's gamble to dress up for the *Heartbeat* audition certainly paid dividends. 'I thought I'd really try and look the Sixties part so I turned up in a mini skirt and big earrings. I was thrilled to get it. I still wear some of my own clothes as Gina — particularly the mini skirts — although other items like her pink leather jacket are on hire.

'At first I wasn't too keen on the clothes I had to wear but I've grown to like them. The only trouble is when we're filming out on the moors it's very cold and I can't get away with wearing thermals underneath because Gina's clothes are so

skimpy there's nowhere to hide them! So my legs freeze and go blue. Luckily most of the time I'm in the warmth of the pub.

'I used to collect glasses in a pub when I was young so I've had some experience of bar work. And I'm much better at pulling pints than when I first started. The heads on the pints used to be huge but I've learned how to tilt the glass.'

KAZIA PELKA as MAGGIE BOLTON

Kazia Pelka is never short of expert advice for her portrayal of District Nurse Maggie Bolton. 'My family has a strong medical background. My grandfather, Randal Herley, was a pioneering eye surgeon in the north and my aunt and uncle are both doctors — one's a paediatrician, the other's a gynaecologist. At one point I thought about becoming a doctor myself but I opted for acting instead.

'In fact I had wanted to act from the moment I appeared in a school play at the age of five. Then I went to a convent school in Leeds where the nuns encouraged drama.'

Prior to *Heartbeat*, Kazia was best known for her stint as Anna Wolska in *Brookside*. 'Some years ago I did a series for Yorkshire Television called *How We Used To Live* which was produced by Carol Wilks and it so happened that she was producing series five of *Heartbeat*. And I'd also recently screen-tested for Keith Richardson as a barmaid at the Woolpack for *Emmerdale*. I didn't get that but I struck lucky with Maggie.

'Maggie's my idea of the ideal nurse. She's very forthright, quite tough and self-reliant because being a rural nurse she has to jump in that Land Rover and drive off alone across the moors. But she's also totally trustworthy with a good sense of irony.

'Back in the Sixties a rural district nurse wore three hats — nurse, midwife and health visitor. So Maggie can poke her nose in — that's her job. In those days people were more likely to confide in a district nurse than in a doctor or the police. I get a lot of help from Sheila Hirst, who was a rural district nurse in the 1960s. She has taught me how to take blood pressure and to use the various instruments. A real bonus was when Maggie got to ride a horse in series eight. I love riding and funnily enough it was the same horse my actor brother

Valentine had ridden in the TV series *Ivanhoe*.

'I also adore Sixties music. I remember as a little girl dancing at home to my mum's singles while she did the housework. My husband — actor/writer Brian Jordan — even buys me *Heartbeat* tapes as stocking fillers at Christmas!'

PETER BENSON as BERNIE SCRIPPS

'Casting directors take one look at me and think undertaker,' laughs Peter Benson who plays Aidensfield garage owner and undertaker Bernie Scripps. 'It must be my lugubrious face. Before Bernie I'd played three undertakers — in *Loot, The Enigma Files* and *Oliver!* At least I'm more qualified to play an undertaker than a garage owner because I'm absolutely clueless about cars. Oil, water, wheels — that's me finished as far as cars are concerned. The crew have a wonderful time with me whenever Bernie is required to do anything remotely complicated. I once tried to clean the air filter with the actual filter.

'I do occasionally get abuse from real garage owners telling me I've done something wrong but most of my public recognition is due to Bernie's association with Greengrass. In London where I live the public are very blasé. If Tom Hanks is in Harrods, everyone just walks past but it's not like that with Greengrass. Scaffolders and taxi drivers are always asking me about Greengrass and Knightsbridge women love him. I was in a carpet store in Sloane Square recently and these very posh women pointed to me and said: "Oh look, there's Greengrass' little friend."

'Visually Bernie and Greengrass are like Laurel and Hardy. There's big Greengrass and there's this little ferret running round after him. Bernie has become Claude's partner-in-crime, something which he usually lives to regret. Bernie is easily led and whilst Claude is his mainstay, Bernie feels overpowered by him. I think Bernie probably lives with mum but is a bit of a goer on the side in Whitby where he has an assortment of barmaid girlfriends.'

Wallasey-born Peter has made his name as a classical actor. He played The Dauphin in the BBC production of 'St. Joan', Henry VI in the BBC Shakespeare series and worked

with Bill Maynard back in 1976 in Alan Plater's "Trinity Tales". However he concedes that before *Heartbeat* he was probably best known as Larry from *Albion Market*.

'I also appeared as Henry VII in the very first episode of *Blackadder*. I'd been playing Henry VI at the BBC when I got a message from producer John Lloyd in the light entertainment department downstairs, saying: "You've done Henry VI, do you want to come down and do Henry VII?" So I did.'

DAVID LONSDALE as DAVID STOCKWELL

David Lonsdale is unlikely ever to forget his debut on *Heartbeat*. 'I had my hand up a dead badger's bottom and was pulling a string to wiggle its tongue. It was for a story in series three about badger baiting. I was going to handle a live badger but the handler said: "On a good day it will leave you alone; on a bad day it will bite off your nose." So we used a stuffed one instead and used strings to make it look alive.

'I seem to get all the animal-handling jobs on the show. I've stuffed worms down a mole hill, held ferrets and in one episode we had a llama. I was assured that because it had been castrated, it wouldn't spit at me and thankfully it didn't.

'I get all the dirty work because David has to do Greengrass' digging. I spent a month last year in a hole full of water, most of the time up to my ankles in mud. If I hadn't kept moving I'd have had moss growing on my north side...'

As a boy, David attended drama classes in his native Southport and at 14 appeared in *Brideshead Revisited*. He was going to study economics at university but ended up going to drama school in London instead. Since then he has worked steadily, including roles as Ken Barlow's son Peter in *Coronation Street* and as a repossession man in *The Full Monty*. 'I enjoy telling people I had a small part in *The Full Monty*,' he grins.

Thirty-six-year-old David, who is married to teacher Diane (they have a daughter Annie, 5, and son Jamie, 2), says of David Stockwell: 'He leads a solitary existence out in the wood where he lives with his mum and is very gullible and in need of looking after. Greengrass has taken him under his wing and treats him like a son. At first David wouldn't go in the shops or the pub but, with Greengrass' tuition, he's become a bit more worldly-wise.

'At the interview for the part, he was described as a naïve country boy. Then when I turned up for my first read through, everyone asked: "Are you playing the idiot?" I didn't take it personally.'

FIONA DOLMAN as JACKIE LAMBERT

Fiona Dolman's most embarrassing *Heartbeat* moment occurred before she had even appeared on screen. 'I was out filming with Kazia one day and there were lots of schoolchildren watching,' recalls Fiona. 'Since this was before my first episode went out, none of them knew who I was. The location manager turned to me and said, "Go and give them your autograph", but I said, "No, they don't know who I am." He disappeared and a few minutes later a horde of children came running over to me and said: "Can we have your autograph? You're Fiona Fullerton, aren't you?" I said, "Who told you that?" They said, "That man", pointing to the location manager. He'd stitched me up.'

Fiona was born at Findhorn in Scotland. 'My dad was in the RAF so we got posted around a lot. I went to boarding school where we did plays once a year and where I had an inspirational English teacher. I was intending to go to university but I couldn't face the thought of more exams so I applied to drama school. That was eight years ago and I've been lucky since.'

Fiona's subsequent credits included *The Good Guys*, *Strike Force*, *A Touch of Frost* and *The Knock*. Fiona says: 'Gerry Poulson, who directs some episodes of *Heartbeat*, had seen me in *Strike Force* and cast me as Jackie from that. My brother's family are big fans of *Heartbeat* so I had watched it whenever I'd stayed with them. I'd also got some of the CDs because I love the music. I met Jason Durr for the first time five minutes before the read through and then I went straight into make-up and into our first scene together.

'Jackie came to Aidensfield to work for her uncle and at first she was keen to let everyone know she wasn't getting a free ride. She was out to prove that she was a solicitor in her own right and was pretty strident in her opinions. There weren't many women solicitors around then and also, being a city girl, I think she felt a bit out of things. But now she's more relaxed and has made friends — especially with Mike.

'Before I played Jackie, I knew nothing about solicitors but my flatmate's father's friend (!) was a lawyer in the 1960s and told me about the type of cases you'd get and the training you'd have.'

Fiona does have one other claim to fame — in 1986 and 1987 she was the RAF Gibraltar ladies' windsurfing champion. It's almost worth an autograph!

VILLAGE HIT BY FOOD POISONING SCARE

— Homemade Horseradish To Blame

A bowl of homemade horseradish was at the root of a food poisoning crisis which put three Aidensfield people in hospital this week.

Frances Parsons and John Dixon, both from Moor Lane, Aidensfield, and Gina Ward, licensee of the Aidensfield Arms, were all rushed to Ashfordly Hospital on Monday, victims of a mystery illness.

ONE MAN'S MEAT ...

Miss Ward was found lying on the kitchen floor of the inn by P.C. Mike Bradley and District Nurse Maggie Bolton. When a case of food poisoning was diagnosed, food samples were taken from the premises and the source was narrowed down to a tray of beef sandwiches.

Other customers had eaten the sandwiches without any ill-effects but a further examination of the kitchen unearthed two batches of horseradish. Alongside an empty jar of manufactured horseradish was a bowl containing a homemade concoction.

POISONOUS ROOT

The roots for the latter had been collected by village gardener David Stockwell but, after consulting his botanical books, Aidensfield G.P. Dr. Neil Bolton discovered that Mr. Stockwell had mixed up poisonous monkshood roots with horseradish roots. Dr. Bolton concluded that the patients were suffering from aconite poisoning.

All three patients have since made a full recovery.

Gina Ward, licensee of the Aidensfield Arms.

FOURTH MAN CHARGED

A fourth man has been charged in connection with the raid on Aidensfield Post Office on 1 August in which over £800 was stolen. Postman Fred Pearson of Long Lane, Whitby, was remanded in custody charged with conspiracy to rob. Mitzy and Johnny Wyler and Jimmy Turpin, all from Rochdale, Lancashire, are already awaiting trial.

FORMER LANDLORD DIES

George Ward, former landlord of the Aidensfield Arms, died this week at the age of 64. He retired from the public house in February and has been ill for some time.

THE WORLD ABOUT US

– The major banks announced that they will close on Saturdays from next July.

– A two-tier post was introduced. A first-class letter costs 5d, a second-class letter costs 4d.

– South Africa cancelled this winter's MCC tour over the tourists' inclusion of England's Cape Coloured cricketer Basil d'Oliveira.

– Scientists announced a new method of relieving pain during childbirth. It is called the epidural technique.

Ashfordly Gazette

With which is incorporated the "Ashfordly Times and North Yorkshire Advertiser"

Registered at the General Post Office as a Newspaper   Established 1856 No. 5884.   Printed and Published by HORNE & SON. LIMITED. WHITBY   FRIDAY, DECEMBER 6th, 1968.   12 Pages.   Price 4 d.   Tel. 396 (Editorial Tel. 1070)

AIDENSFIELD EDITION

MISSING ISOTOPE HUNT ENDS IN CLIFF RESCUE

Possible Disaster Averted —

A car theft from outside the Aidensfield Arms yesterday lunchtime sparked a dramatic hunt across North Yorkshire for a potentially deadly radioactive atomic isotope. The search eventually went full circle back near Aidensfield to the beauty spot of Sillers Drop where a youth carrying the isotope fell over the edge of a cliff. The boy and the isotope were both recovered intact.

ALARMING

The alarm was raised by nuclear power station employee Alec Formby who reported that his Mini car had been stolen from outside the Aidensfield Arms while he had been having lunch with his girlfriend. Mr. Formby told the police that in the boot of the car, in a wooden box, was an atomic Isotope. He warned that if the isotope was removed from its protective casing, it would cause death by irradiation.

'The isotope was contained in a lead flask,' said Mr. Formby, 'and one of my many fears was that kids would find it and think it contained hot soup.'

POTENTIAL KILLER

Responding to the alert, Sgt. Raymond Craddock of Ashfordly Police arranged for the BBC to broadcast a radio warning about the atomic isotope. Anyone coming across the package was instructed not to touch it on any account but to

(continued on page 4)

Ex-police Sergeant Oscar Blaketon (left) with Trevor and Stuart Chivers.

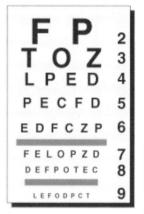

NUCLEAR ALERT

(continued from page 1)

Trevor Chivers shows off the isotope to David Stockwell and Claude Jeremiah Greengrass.

notify the police immediately. Sgt. Craddock also enlisted the expert assistance of Mr. Roger Farrington from the Radiology Protection Service. With every police officer in the area involved in the hunt for the stolen Mini, it was reported to have crashed near Elsinby. But by the time the police and Mr. Farrington arrived, the car had vanished once more.

The driver was thought to have been hurt in the crash and when District Nurse Maggie Bolton saw William Reynolds, a known car thief, being treated for injuries in Ashfordly Hospital, she notified the police. Reynolds admitted stealing the car and said that it had been taken to an Aidensfield scrap yard.

EMPTY

At the yard, police found the car but no sign of the isotope which had been removed from its wooden box. As fears mounted by the minute, officers visited local schools to describe the isotope and to warn children about the danger of tampering with it.

Unbeknown to the police, the lead flask containing the isotope had been taken from the car yard by local youths Trevor and Stuart Chivers who were planning to sell it for scrap. They tried to do a deal for the flask and a quantity of old copper with Aidensfield dealer Claude Jeremiah Greengrass but he put it in his shed and told them to come back later.

When Trevor Chivers realised what they had taken, he retrieved it from Mr. Greengrass's shed and threatened to explode it after school.

GREENGRASS TO THE RESCUE

Mr. Greengrass recognised the description of the missing isotope on the radio and, after searching his shed,

informed P.C. Mike Bradley that the Chivers' lads had got it.

Stuart Chivers was worried about his brother's plan and told the police that Trevor intended to explode the isotope in front of friends up at Sillers Drop. Officers raced to the scene but Trevor ran off. In his haste to escape, he fell over the cliff edge and landed on a ledge some 20 feet below. P.C. Bradley was winched down to rescue him. To the relief of all concerned, the isotope was undamaged.

EMPTY

Afterwards Sgt. Craddock told the *Gazette*: 'I am pleased to report that the efficient operation conducted by Ashfordly Police has resulted in the safe recovery of the atomic isotope and the aversion of a potentially major catastrophe.'

Two local men are expected to be charged with car theft.

WRECKED CAR SCAM EXPOSED
— Local Dealer Charged

Ann and Ken Marsden.

Aidensfield car dealer Ken Marsden appeared before Ashfordly Magistrates yesterday charged with knowingly re-selling cars that had been written off. He was bailed to reappear in a month's time. Also charged was Vic Owens, an insurance assessor from Redcar.

The alleged racket came to light following a near-fatal car crash last week. Mr. Brian Rider of Denby Close, Aidensfield, had recently bought a second-hand Lotus Cortina from Mr. Marsden's showrooms and was taking it out for a spin on Friday afternoon when the car crashed into a tree on the Strensford road.

MORE FIRES

The badly-damaged car was brought back to Bernie Scipps' garage in Aidensfield where it mysteriously caught fire and exploded in a ball of flames.

Mr. Rider's mother, Jean, claimed that Mr. Marsden had deliberately set fire to the car to destroy the evidence. She added that even before the crash her son had complained about the car's defective steering.

The police suspected that Mrs. Ann Marsden was covering up for her husband but, despite evidence that he had been hitting her, she refused to get involved.

ABUSE

District Nurse Maggie Bolton said: 'There was heavy bruising on Mrs. Marsden's back and shoulders and she also had a sprained wrist. It was obvious that someone was beating her but she wouldn't press charges against her husband.'

However Mrs. Marsden soon had a change of heart. According to the police, Mr. Marsden was seeing another woman and when his wife challenged him about it, he turned on her again. This time a tearful Mrs. Marsden ran to the Aidensfield Police House and told P.C. Mike Bradley that her husband was re-selling written-off cars in partnership with Vic Owens.

WIFE PROVIDES INVALUABLE HELP

Volunteering to find out where the written-off cars were being taken for repair, Mrs. Marsden eavesdropped on a conversation between the two men and discovered that collection of another car was planned. Police intercepted the truck towing the wrecked car and Sgt. Raymond Craddock of Ashfordly Police, wearing civilian clothes, took over at the wheel. He drove the tow truck into Mr. Marsden's showrooms and, pretending to be lost, asked for directions to the secret repair workshop. When Mr. Marsden gave him directions, Sgt. Craddock revealed his true identity and arrested him.

Police officers took away seven vehicles from the repair shop for further examination.

Ashfordly Gazette

With which is incorporated the "Ashfordly Times and North Yorkshire Advertiser"

Registered at the General Post Office as a Newspaper — Established 1856 No. 5892. — Printed and Published by HORNE & SON. LIMITED. WHITBY — FRIDAY, JANUARY 31st, 1969. — 12 Pages. — Price 4 d. — Tel. 396 (Editorial Tel. 1070)

AIDENSFIELD EDITION

BANK EMPLOYEE TO STAND TRIAL OVER 1949 DEATH

New Evidence Follows Aidensfield Robbery

Tim McDonald, assistant manager at the Aidensfield branch of the Northern Bank, has been charged with the manslaughter of schoolmate Sean Robinson who plunged to his death in a mine 20 years ago. Although the verdict at the time was death by misadventure, another man, Carl Southall, was widely held responsible.

McDonald's complicity came to light after Southall, also an old school friend, had returned to Aidensfield after being released from prison having served a 12-year sentence for armed robbery. It is claimed that Southall then tried to frame McDonald for a bank raid in the village in revenge for having taken the blame for Sean's death.

INNOCENT BLAMED

The body of 14-year-old Sean Robinson was found at the foot of a shaft at the Old Boar Mines, near Aidensfield, on 11 January 1949. He had been seen playing with Tim McDonald and Carl Southall shortly before his death. Although the Coroner ruled the death to have been accidental, local gossip blamed Southall, a known tearaway. Such were the accusations that his family was forced to leave the district.

While Southall drifted into a life of crime, McDonald earned a respectable living with the Northern Bank, working his way up to assis-

tant manager. Then three weeks ago, on the twentieth anniversary of Sean's death, the Finch Road, Aidensfield, home of McDonald and his wife Jenny was broken into while they were asleep. The only thing taken was an old cricket trophy.

RETURN TO SCENE

Police later discovered the trophy, along with a rucksack containing clothes, at the Old Boar Mines while checking out reports of boys playing there. When Southall returned to collect the rucksack, P.C.s Mike Bradley and Phil Bellamy questioned him about the break-in.

Southall readily admitted it but said that McDonald was an old friend. McDonald confirmed the fact and refused to press charges.

(continued on page 2)

P.C. Phil Bellamy.

P.C. Mike Bradley.

DEATH CHARGE

Sargeant Raymond Craddock oversaw the investigation.

(continued from page 1)

Two nights later, the home of Mrs. Robinson, Sean's mother, was broken into and a shotgun was stolen. Descriptions of the burglar fitted Southall but McDonald provided him with an alibi.

According to McDonald, Southall then began leaning on him to help rob the bank where he worked. If McDonald did not comply, Southall allegedly threatened to harm his wife. He later fired a shot at the McDonalds' kitchen window. Finally Southall threatened to reveal the truth about Sean Robinson's death. Blackmailed into submission, McDonald agreed to draw a layout of the bank.

GUN CRIME

On the morning of 16 January, Southall, armed with a shotgun, burst into the Aidensfield branch of the Northern Bank and escaped in a stolen car with over £1,000. The manager immediately suspected that the robber had inside knowledge.

Knowing of Southall's history of armed robbery, police officers went to question his friend McDonald. A search of McDonald's house revealed a holdall full of bank notes. It was then that McDonald confessed that he had pushed Sean Robinson to his death and that Southall, desperate for revenge after being blamed for the boy's death, was now trying to frame him for the bank robbery.

CHARGES

Southall was arrested the following day in Cheshire and charged with armed robbery and blackmail. McDonald has been charged with the manslaughter of Sean Robinson and with conspiracy to rob. The former school friends will be tried separately.

'HAIR' CUT

The Aidensfield Players' planned forthcoming production of the controversial musical 'Hair' has been scrapped. An official statement cited 'artistic differences' but a source told the *Gazette* that the only person willing to take her clothes off was the prompter — 86-year-old Mildred Braithwaite.

THE WORLD ABOUT US

– Ford unveiled its new sports saloon car, the Capri.

– Northern Ireland Protestant leader Rev. Ian Paisley was jailed for three months for unlawful assembly.

– Police clashed with students at the London School of Economics.

– The BBC announced that its longest-running radio show, 'The Dales', will end in April.

– Fleetwood Mac topped the charts with the haunting instrumental 'Albatross'.

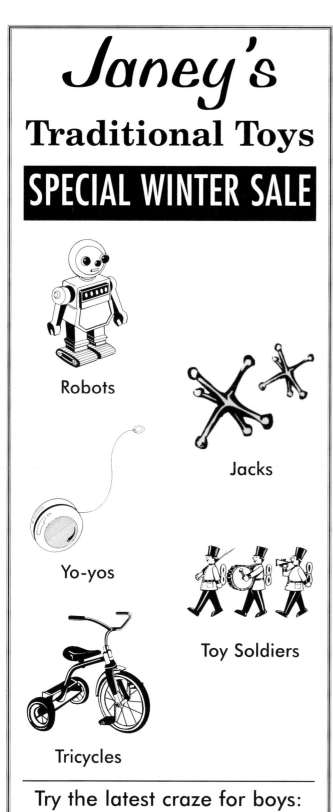
MAGISTRATE INJURED IN CAR CRASH

Victim Of Black Magic?

Ashfordly Police refused to speculate last night on rumours that a road crash which left a local magistrate in hospital was the result of black magic.

Derek Harper's veteran Roadster two-seater swerved off the Eltering road at around 3.30 on Wednesday afternoon, ploughing into a hedge. Mr. Harper suffered serious head injuries and was rushed to Ashfordly Hospital where he is now out of danger. Police investigating the accident found a sack on the passenger seat. Inside the sack was a 300-year-old human skull, believed to have been stolen from a tomb at St. Michael's Church, Eltering, the previous night.

DEVILISH

The vicar of St. Michael's, Rev. Anthony Foyle, said that the thieves had also painted a red pentagram on the door.

The theft was the latest in a series of raids on churches in the area during which a number of crosses and chalices have been taken. Police suspect that a gang of youths are responsible. On Sunday night Oscar Blaketon, postmaster of Aidensfield Post Office, was hit over the head when he disturbed intruders in St. Michael's graveyard.

Three months ago, 70-year-old Henry Follett of Marsh Farm, Eltering, was sent a wax doll after trying to prevent rustlers stealing his sheep. Mr. Follett, who spent much of his life in Africa, reported that the thieves had struck on the same night every month for four months, taking just one animal each time.

LARGE GROUP

One night he waited for the thieves to arrive and followed them. He told the police that the two rustlers were wearing long cloaks and that, after taking the sheep, they drove up on to the moor above the farm where they joined about a dozen colleagues. Mr. Follett then drove his Land Rover straight at them, forcing them to scatter. The following morning he woke up to find the wax doll on his bed.

MUMBO-JUMBO

Asked by the *Gazette* to comment on rumours that witchcraft was rife in the area, Mr. Follett said: 'It's all mumbo-jumbo to you, but I spent a lot of time in the bush with men who believed in and practised magic. I've seen its power.' Mr. Follett declined to elaborate further.

(continued on page 8)

MUD, MUD, INGLORIOUS MUD
— Woman May Sue After Face Pack Horror

Awealthy woman is threatening legal action against an Aidensfield resident after a special facial mud pack he sold her brought her out in ugly blotches.

Mrs. Dorothea Cliveden, 62, of Holme House, Elsinby, was recommended a natural mixture by Claude Jeremiah Greengrass. But when she put it on her face, it caused a hideous red rash.

An angry Mrs. Cliveden told the *Gazette*: 'Greengrass was supposed to be doing some gardening work for me but we got round to talking about cosmetic mud packs. I told him that I used expensive Dead Sea mud on my face to keep my skin looking so young but he told me that local Crackley Mire mud was every bit as good.

ANCIENT BALM

'He spun me some yarn about Lady Ashfordly having discovered it in the last century. He told me that when she died at the age of 80, she still looked like a woman of 45. He said it was the minerals in the mud and that he could supply it to me regularly for a fee.

'Well I wasn't just going to take his word for it so I asked him for a sample in order that I might send it for analysis. The laboratories reported back that it was certainly the equal of Dead Sea mud so, believing it to be the font of eternal youth, I put this seemingly wonderful Crackley Mire mud on my face and then took a bath in it. I haven't dared go out of the house since.

DUD MUD

'Greengrass blamed pollution but I think he's a con man who switched the jars before I sent the mud for analysis. I'm considering taking him to court.'

Asked to comment about Mrs. Cliveden's facial blotches, Mr. Greengrass would only say: 'I think red suits her.'

WITCH SURVEY

(continued from page 6)

Aidensfield's most celebrated witch was Ma Hall who lived on the edge of the moors and was burnt at the stake 400 years ago.

Sgt. Raymond Craddock of Ashfordly Police dismissed the stories: 'Since I have yet to encounter any old hags whistling across moonlit skies on broomsticks, I am treating these rumours with a large pinch of salt. I am confident that the thefts will turn out to be nothing more sinister than the work of errant youngsters.'

Claude Jeremiah Greengrass.

POLICE RAID WITCHES' COVEN

Police investigating a series of church thefts and a car crash which put magistrate Derek Harper in hospital raided a witches' coven at the Black Knights Stone Circle on Tuesday night. One man, Robert Hall, was later charged with intimidation, theft and sheep rustling.

The breakthrough in the case came when officers tracked down Mr. Harper's 17-year-old son Simon who confessed to having once been a member of a coven run by Robert Hall. Simon Harper said that he had found a human skull stolen from a tomb at St. Michael's Church, Eltering. The skull was later discovered in his father's crashed car.

STOLEN SKULL

Derek Harper, thinking that his son was involved in the theft, had been on his way to hand the skull in to Ashfordly Police Station.

Simon Harper claimed that the skull had been stolen from the church by Hall for use in the initiation ceremony of Harper's sister Sally. He was afraid that Hall had used witchcraft to harm his father out of revenge, Hall having been severely dealt with by Mr. Harper when appearing before him in court. However police confirmed that the road accident was caused by faulty brakes.

WAX WORKS

Simon Harper also alleged that a wax doll had been sent by Hall to farmer Henry Follett to scare him off. Mr. Follett had earlier spotted members of the coven stealing his sheep.

Acting on information received, police officers swooped on the coven meeting and arrested Hall.

One of the officers involved in the raid, P.C. Phil Bellamy, said: 'It was dead spooky. There was a lot of smoke and all these figures in long robes in a semi-circle. In the middle was a girl on her knees. You just don't think of things like that going on close to home — I always thought the only person who went out wandering at night around here was that Claude Jeremiah Greengrass.'

VALENTINE'S DANCE

A Valentine's Day Dance will take place at Aidensfield Village Hall tonight at 7.30. Music is by Ronnie Rock and the Rockets and admission is 3s 6d.

MISSING WOMAN FOUND IN FARMHOUSE

— Baker's Man Held

Melanie Drinkwater, the Aidensfield woman missing for five days, was found safe and well after police raided a remote farmhouse on Saturday. Barry Hadfield, a delivery man at the bakery where Miss Drinkwater worked, was later charged with abduction and false imprisonment. He is due to appear before Ashfordly Magistrates on Monday.

Miss Drinkwater left her home in Moor Lane, Aidensfield, on the evening of Monday 24 February after packing an overnight bag and telling her mother that she was going to stay with her best friend, Karen Reilly. However, she was secretly planning to elope to Gretna Green that night with her boyfriend Terry Phillips.

After meeting up with Miss Reilly, who gave her a wedding present, she set off to meet Mr. Phillips in a country lane as arranged. But when Mr. Phillips arrived in his car, there was no sign of her.

Her family were not unduly worried when she failed to turn up for work at Aidensfield Bakery the following morning. Her mother had suspected that she was about to elope and assumed that she had gone through with it. It was only when Mr. Phillips came forward to report her missing that fears grew for her safety.

Mr. Phillips immediately challenged her former boyfriend, Michael Davies, who had been seen hanging around outside the bakery on the evening of the 24th. He had apparently offered Miss Drinkwater a lift home but she had refused his offer. Davies denied knowing anything about her abduction.

The police subsequently questioned Davies but he produced an alibi for the night of Miss Drinkwater's disappearance. However

District Nurse Maggie Bolton and her husband, Dr. Neil Bolton, led police to the farmhouse.

Miss Reilly told officers that Davies and a friend, Keith Winstanley, had once tried to get her and Miss Drinkwater drunk by spiking their wine. The police discovered that Davies had a record for drug dealing and when his alibi proved to be false, they quizzed him again.

(continued on page 5)

WOMAN FOUND

(continued from page 2)

This time he admitted that he and Winstanley were responsible for breaking in to Dr. Neil Bolton's Aidensfield surgery on the evening Miss Drinkwater disappeared but again denied kidnapping her.

As the hunt intensified and concern mounted, P.C. Mike Bradley casually chatted to delivery man Hadfield about the case. During the course of their conversation, Hadfield dropped a ring box and said that he was engaged to a girl called Jeanie Walsh.

But when P.C. Bradley discovered that 'Jeanie Walsh' was the name of a shop, he became suspicious, especially when Sue Driscoll, a clerical assistant at Ashfordly Police Station, revealed that Hadfield had told her that his fiancee's name was Melanie.

MEDICAL RECORD

District Nurse Maggie Bolton had also been concerned that Hadfield had failed to keep an appointment with her husband for treatment for severe headaches. She and Dr. Bolton arrived at Hadfield's house to find the police already there. Mrs. Bolton then recalled an isolated farmhouse once owned by Hadfield's parents. There police found Hadfield and the captive Miss Drinkwater. Although physically unharmed, she was found in a distressed condition.

HER STORY

She was able to recount her ordeal to the *Gazette* on Wednesday. 'I had been waiting to meet Terry in the lane and when I saw a car coming, I assumed it was him. It was difficult to see properly — I was blinded by the headlights. It wasn't until I was half in that I saw that the driver was Barry Hadfield.

'I tried to get out but he dragged me in and locked the door. He didn't say much — he just drove me around these dark lanes. I kept looking out for landmarks or lights, but there weren't any. It was just so dark. He drove for about a quarter of an hour — it seemed like an eternity — until we reached a house.

'He marched me upstairs and locked me in a bedroom. He brought me food and drink from time to time and I tried to reason with him, to find out why he was doing this to me. He told me he thought I loved him because I'd sent him a Valentine card years ago. I told him I was about to marry someone else but he didn't want to know.

'At one point I tried to escape but just when I thought he wasn't around, he suddenly reappeared. Then he blindfolded me and took me to another house where he said he was sure we would live happily together. He didn't hurt me or anything — he just seemed to want to keep me as his possession.'

(continued on page 6)

Mr Claude Jeremiah Greengrass, (left) and his dog, Alfred.

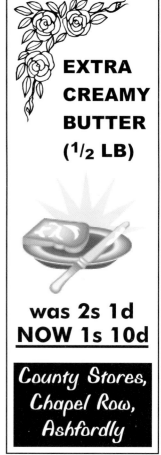
FLEA MARKET

A roadside stall selling sheepskin rugs has been closed down by health inspectors after the rugs were found to be infested with fleas. Officials moved in following complaints from over 30 people claiming to have been bitten.

Victims included Aidensfield postmaster Oscar Blaketon. He told the *Gazette*: 'I was scratching my head trying to work out how the fleas could have got into my house. The only thing I had bought recently was a sheepskin rug so I was itching to get my hands on the person who had sold it to me.'

The offending stallholder, local businessman Claude Jeremiah Greengrass, thinks that his dog Alfred must have slept on the rugs. 'Not that there's anything unhygienic or dirty about Alfred,' said Mr. Greengrass. 'It's because he's so clean and has got such lovely soft fur that the fleas must have chosen him. For them, it's like staying at the Savoy Hotel.

'But I'm sick as a budgie,' he added. 'Those rugs were my best-selling line. Not only that but I've discovered that my assistant had been underpricing them. How's a bloke supposed to make an honest living?'

ABDUCTION

(continued from page 5)

'I just kept hoping that someone would come for me. Thank God they did in the end.

'When I was released I just wanted to see my mum and dad and Terry because I thought I'd never see them again. My mum hugged me and I said I was sorry for all the grief I'd caused her. I didn't want any more rows so I agreed to put back my wedding plans. When I do get married I've decided I want all my family there, not just a low-key ceremony with a couple of strangers as witnesses. That's the one positive thing that's come out of all this.'

THE WORLD ABOUT US

– The Kray twins were given life sentences after being found guilty of murder.

– Preparations continued for the official opening of London's new Underground line, the Victoria Line.

– The French Concorde made its maiden flight. The British plane is expected to follow suit next month.

MYSTERY OF CYCLIST'S DEATH
— Body Dumped By Roadside

First on the scene: P.C.s Mike Bradley and Phil Bellamy.

Ashfordly Police confessed yesterday to being still baffled by the circumstances surrounding the death of racing cyclist Paolo Ermini whose body was found in a gully on the Whitby road on Wednesday morning. Foul play has not been ruled out.

The corpse of Mr. Ermini, 35, a member of York Bantams Cycling Club, was discovered by P.C.s Mike Bradley and Phil Bellamy near Paddocks Cross. It was half-hidden from view by a rocky outcrop. Examining the body, which was lying in an awkward position, Dr. Neil Bolton noted extensive bruising, lacerations, burns on the arm and a broken neck. The dead man's shoes were also on the wrong feet. There was no sign of his bicycle.

The first indications were that he may have fallen from his machine but the position of the body led Dr. Bolton to speculate another cause of death and the possibility that the victim may have died elsewhere.

CLUES AT SCENE

Sgt. Raymond Craddock recognised the specialist blue cycling shirt as being of Italian origin and when Mr. Ermini was reported missing, the victim was duly identified by his wife Lizzie. Police then began conducting a search for the missing bicycle and photographed a number of tyre tracks found at the scene.

They also studied a piece of material found snagged on a nearby fence.

Probing the deceased's background to see whether he had any enemies, the police learned that a few club members were jealous of his success. His fiercest rival was Tony Eccles who had once been engaged to the future Mrs. Ermini. Mr. Eccles is expected to be questioned soon.

MOTIVES

'There are one or two possible motives, but nothing concrete,' said Sgt. Craddock yesterday. 'It remains something of a puzzle. Anyway until we get the post-mortem results, we are keeping an open mind.'

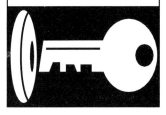

CYCLIST DIED AFTER RUG LOVE-IN

— Heart Attack Verdict

The death of Italian racing cyclist Paolo Ermini, whose body was found in a roadside gully near Paddocks Cross nine days ago, was the result of a passionate fireside encounter, Ashfordly Police revealed this week.

Police had been treating the death of Mr. Ermini as suspicious after matching a fragment of clothing found on a fence at the scene to a jacket found to be worn by local man Barry Watson. Tyre marks found close to the body were identical to those on Mr. Watson's van.

However the eagerly-awaited post-mortem showed that Mr. Ermini had died from a heart attack. The pathologist also stated that the burns on the dead man's arm were made by an electric fire and that the body had been moved after death.

ON THE JOB

With Mr. Watson the number one suspect, his wife Millie came forward to reveal the true nature of the Italian's death. She disclosed that she and Mr. Ermini had been having a weekly affair while her husband played darts and that her lover had died on the rug during a session of lovemaking.

She told the police: 'He threw out his arm and he kind of gasped. But in the circumstances I thought … Then I smelt burning and I saw his poor arm was on the electric fire. First I panicked.

Sgt. Raymond Craddock of Ashfordly Police.

Then I cried. Then I calmed down. I dressed him and got him and his bike into Barry's truck. I drove up on to the moors. I thought I could make it look more like an accident.

'I was wearing Barry's jacket — that's how a scrap ended up on the fence.'

RUG ADDICT

Sgt. Raymond Craddock said: 'Mrs. Watson added that she had only bought the fateful rug by accident. She was at an auction and thought she was bidding for a view of Fountains Abbey. Even so, she felt that she had got her money's worth.'

'UFO' WAS CARGO PLANE

A reported UFO sighting last week has turned out to be nothing more alien than a cargo plane. The claim of a flying saucer by farmer Ned Hall was the latest in a series of suspected sightings in the Aidensfield area. He described a dark silent shape overhead but police investigations showed the craft to be a cargo plane on a run from Leeds to Edinburgh. Two pilots have apparently been defying regulations by switching off their engines to see how far they can glide.

Ashfordly Gazette

With which is incorporated the "Ashfordly Times and North Yorkshire Advertiser"

Registered at the General Post Office as a Newspaper. | Established 1856 No. 5905. | Printed and Published by HORNE & SON, LIMITED, WHITBY. | FRIDAY, MAY 2nd, 1969. | 12 Pages. | Price 4 d. | Tel. 396 (Editorial Tel. 1070)

AIDENSFIELD EDITION

HERO P.C. SAVES VILLAGE

— Catastrophe Averted

P.C. Mike Bradley was the toast of Aidensfield last night after freeing a lorry-load of deadly chemicals from beneath a railway bridge and then driving it away from houses and into a field. Seconds after he jumped clear, the lorry exploded into a ball of flames.

LUCKY ESCAPE FOR VILLAGE

If the explosion had taken place nearer the village, there would probably have been fatalities and undoubtedly many casualties.

The incident occurred when Aidensfield factory owner Colin Horton, suspected of dumping chemicals illegally, drove one of his lorries out of the gates as the police were about to question him. A quarter of a mile down the Ashfordly road, the lorry became wedged under a low railway bridge.

The collision caused the lorry's load of drums to be crushed and their contents began leaking ominously.

P.C. Bradley was first to arrive on the scene and instantly recognised that if the lorry's punctured fuel tank caught fire and mixed with the leaking chemicals, the resulting explosion would cause devastation in the immediate vicinity.

STROKE OF GENIUS SAVES THE DAY

With Mr. Horton himself badly injured by the crash, it was left to P.C. Bradley to try and drive the vehicle clear of the bridge. Despite repeated

Laden with deadly chemicals, the lorry trapped under the Ashfordly bridge.

attempts, the lorry would not shift. It was stuck fast.

With time running out, P.C. Bradley had a stroke of inspiration and decided to let down the tyres. This had the effect of lowering the roof of the lorry cab and enabling the vehicle to be driven away from the bridge.

Driver Colin Horton was badly injured and is expected to miss tomorrow's rugby match between Aidensfield Seconds and Old Ashfordlians Fifths.

He may also face criminal charges.

(continued on page 2)

POLICE HERO

(continued from page 1)

Aware that he was at the wheel of a time bomb, P.C. Bradley steered the ailing lorry away from the village and drove it into a field behind Aidensfield Football Ground. He then leaped from the cab, moments before the entire lorry burst into flames and exploded.

Thanks to P.C. Bradley's actions, the only injury was Mr. Horton. The officer himself emerged unscathed.

JUST A JOB

Last night Sgt. Raymond Craddock of Ashfordly Police said of P.C. Bradley who has been based at the Police House in Aidensfield for the past year: 'It was good work, using a deal of initiative. But it was no more than we would expect from one of our officers.'

The explosion marked the culmination of two weeks of controversy surrounding Horton's. Villagers had become increasingly alarmed by the number of heavy lorries rumbling through Aidensfield to the newly-opened factory. Many of the complainants were elderly, kept awake by the constant stream of late-night deliveries.

With the police powerless to act, the pensioners took the law into their own hands and on Tuesday evening formed a human barrier designed to prevent lorries from entering the factory. Ironically one of the most active protesters was the grandmother of P.C. Phil Bellamy, stationed at Ashfordly.

FISHY CHEMICAL COCKTAIL

Mr. Horton promptly called the police and explained that the lorries were bringing in material to fill in old mine shafts in the factory. When police were alerted to tens of dead fish found at Torley Bottoms in a stream which passes close to the factory, Mr. Horton vehemently denied using pesticides or dumping chemicals into the stream.

But P.C. Bradley remained unconvinced, particularly when local youth Trevor Chivers reported seeing some metal drums stacked inside Horton's factory. Nor were the protesters appeased and Granny Bellamy elected to handcuff herself to the factory gates.

(continued on page 4)

LORRY EXPLOSION

(continued from page 2)

While P.C. Bellamy dealt with the aged militant, P.C. Bradley noticed a lorry loaded with drums standing inside the gates. Their presence supported the theory that the factory was practising illegal dumping. According to unconfirmed sources, Mr. Horton's driver then walked out after being refused danger money for dumping the remaining chemicals, leaving Mr. Horton to do the job himself. Ignorant of the usual route, he drove straight under the low bridge.

Police last night confirmed that the stream had been poisoned by chemicals leaking out of the old mine shafts. Mr. Horton is expected to be charged in connection with the matter today.

THE WORLD ABOUT US

– Manchester City defeated Leicester City 1–0 in the FA Cup final.

– General de Gaulle resigned as French President.

– Terence O'Neill resigned as Prime Minister of Northern Ireland in the wake of disturbances in Belfast and Londonderry.

– 500 more British troops were sent to Northern Ireland to guard key installations.

TV HIGHLIGHTS

TONIGHT. *Hark at Barker* (ITV, 10.30pm). Aristocratic comedy starring Ronnie Barker as Lord Rustless and David Jason as his decrepit gardener Dithers.

SATURDAY. *The Avengers* (ITV, 8.15pm). Mother suspects that Tara King is selling secrets to the enemy. Steed has 24 hours to prove her innocence.

SUNDAY. *The Golden Shot* (ITV, 4.30pm). Bob Monkhouse hosts another edition of the crossbow-shooting game show. With Anne Aston.

SUNDAY. *Dr. Finlay's Casebook* (BBC, 8pm). Dr. Snoddy falls out with Dr. Cameron over the treatment of a patient.

SUNDAY. *Department S* (ITV, 8.30pm). Jason, Stewart and Annabelle look into a car crash with a tailor's dummy at the wheel. Starring Peter Wyngarde, Joel Fabiani and Rosemary Nicols.

MONDAY. *Coronation Street* (ITV, 7.30pm). Annie Walker enters a Perfect Landlady competition.

MONDAY. *Q5* (BBC2, 8.50pm). More lunacy with Spike Milligan. Last of series.

WEDNESDAY. *The Mind of Mr. J.G. Reeder* (ITV, 9pm). Reeder investigates the theft of the emeralds of Suleiman the Magnificent. Starring Hugh Burden.

WEDNESDAY. *Sez Les* (ITV, 10.30pm). Comedy with Les Dawson.

FOOTPATH PROTEST ENDS IN POLICE CHASE

Demonstrators Charged Over Bank Robbery —

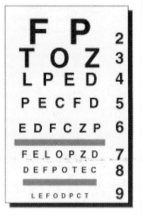

Sgt. Raymond Craddock tries to defuse the situation.

W hat started out as a peaceful protest about the closure of a public footpath turned into a dramatic police hunt across the North York Moors in search of a gang of bank robbers.

Last night husband and wife Ronald and Doreen Tidy were charged by Newcastle upon Tyne police in connection with the raid at a branch of the Tyneside Bank in the city in 1958. A third person, Barry Dixon, has already served a ten-year sentence for the robbery.

WALKING HOLIDAY

The Tidys booked into the Aidensfield Arms last Friday and announced that they were on a walking holiday. They said they were planning a hiking expedition to the Upper Esk waterfall a mile off the Strensford road. However Mary Ward, sister of late licensee George Ward and aunt of the present incumbent, the divine Gina Ward, had discovered that Lord Ashfordly had closed the right of way leading to the waterfall.

Undeterred, the Tidys set off on their intended journey the following morning, ignoring Lord Ashfordly's 'Keep Out' signs on the footpath until they were stopped by His Lordship's gamekeepers. As tempers became frayed, Ronald Tidy was bitten by one of the gamekeepers' dogs.

PUBLIC SUPPORT

He took his injuries and his tale of oppression to Dr. Neil Bolton who thought it outrageous that Lord Ashfordly should close the path to the public. As a show of support, Dr. Bolton and his wife, District Nurse Maggie Bolton, said they would join the Tidys on a protest walk along the footpath on Sunday morning. When Lord Ashfordly's gamekeepers challenged the 'trespassers', P.C. Mike Bradley and P.C. Alfred Ventress stepped in to defuse the situation.

POLICE TROUBLE

The police wanted to question the Tidys about a brick which was thrown through a window at the head gamekeeper's cottage the previous day, following the incident with the dog. However there was insufficient evidence to hold them and they were released.

(continued on page 9)

PROTEST MARCH

Ronald Tidy (left) leads the protestors in a sing-a-long.

(continued from page 2)

In the meantime Barry Dixon had also arrived in Aidensfield, having been freed from prison. His every move was shadowed by Ed Baxter who had been employed by an insurance company to recover the money stolen in the Newcastle bank robbery. Dixon complained to Sgt. Raymond Craddock of Ashfordly Police that he was being harassed by Mr. Baxter but Sgt. Craddock gave him short shrift.

UNDERTAKING WORK

Dixon landed a job as a grave digger with Aidensfield undertaker Bernie Scripps but word reached the police that Dixon was only back in Aidensfield to collect the proceeds from the robbery. The stolen money had never been found but was thought to have been hidden somewhere in the Aidensfield area.

By now feeling in the village was running high about the closed footpath and Dr. Bolton and Tidy organised a full-scale protest for Tuesday morning. A coach was laid on to transport over 50 demonstrators to Lord Ashfordly's estate. Waiting at the footpath were Lord Ashfordly's gamekeepers and a posse of policemen.

FLATFOOT'S FLAT

P.C. Bradley had intend following the protesters' coach by car but a flat tyre delayed his departure. However his suspicions had already been aroused about the true purpose of the Tidys' visit to Aidensfield.

'When they were released earlier, I casually asked Mrs. Tidy about one of the badges on her haversack,' P.C. Bradley told the *Gazette*, 'and I couldn't help but notice her hesitation. That struck me as odd considering she claimed to be an avid walker and I began to wonder whether she was all that she seemed. So I checked out the address they had given when booking in at the Aidensfield Arms and found it to be false. I made further inquiries and received a message back from Newcastle Police that Ronald Tidy was wanted for bank robbery.'The coach arrived at Lord Ashfordly's stables shortly before mid-day and blocked the entrance. The police and Lord Ashfordly's men heard about the blockade, realised they were in the wrong place and rushed to the stables.

(continued on page 10)

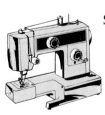

POLICE CHASE

Protestors against Lord Ashfordly's restrictions of right of way.

(continued from page 9)

Dixon, who is believed to have made a secret phone call to Tidy to arrange a rendezvous, escaped from Mr. Baxter's watchful gaze by stealing his motorcycle. P.C. Bradley put two and two together and, joined by Mr. Baxter, followed Dixon in the police car.

REAL REASON FOR PROTEST

With Lord Ashfordly's men and the police having deserted the footpath for the stables, Dixon's route to the waterfall was unhindered. Ronald Tidy now slipped away from the protest group at the stables and was picked up in a car by his wife and driven out towards the waterfall. But when they saw the parked police car, they decided against joining Dixon.

P.C. Bradley and Mr. Baxter followed Dixon all the way to the waterfall and saw him retrieve the money from his hiding place. When confronted by Mr. Baxter, Dixon simply tossed the money into the water.

The Tidys were picked up later that afternoon when they tried to return to the Aidensfield Arms. They were then taken to Newcastle Police Station where they were charged on counts of robbery.

JOB TIDIED UP NICELY

Like the rest of the village, Gina Ward was stunned to hear that the Tidys were criminals. 'They seemed such a normal couple,' she said.

Yesterday Lord Ashfordly agreed to re-open the disputed right of way after the study of old maps revealed that he had built over a number of public footpaths.

BLACK WEDDING

A bride's big day was ruined when the chimney sweep she had hired to bring her good luck instead brought nothing but misfortune. Glenda Whitlow of Hereford Road, Elsinby, was mortified when the sweep's dog showered her beautiful, white wedding dress with soot. The wedding guests looked on aghast. Even the cake was in tiers.

After the wedding at St. Matthew's Church, Elsinby, the groom, Alan Rashley, stormed: 'Instead of looking like a beautiful virginal bride, my wife looked like an extra from *101 Dalmatians*.'

The 'lucky' sweep, Aidensfield man Claude Jeremiah Greengrass, was believed to be in hiding.

THE WORLD ABOUT US

– A Coroner concluded that Rolling Stone Brian Jones, who drowned in his swimming pool on 2 July, died from a mixture of alcohol and drugs.

– Prince Charles carried out his first duties since his investiture as Prince of Wales on 1 July.

– Thunderclap Newman topped the charts with 'Something in the Air'.

– Ann Jones became only the second Briton since the war to win the ladies' singles title at Wimbledon.

– The BBC launched a new American science fiction series to be screened from tomorrow. It is called *Star Trek*.

Ashfordly Gazette

With which is incorporated the "Ashfordly Times and North Yorkshire Advertiser"

Registered at the General Post Office as a Newspaper. | Established 1856 No. 5917. | Printed and Published by HORNE & SON. LIMITED. WHITBY | FRIDAY, JULY 25th, 1969. | 12 Pages. | Price 4d. | Tel. 396 (Editorial Tel. 1070)

AIDENSFIELD EDITION

AIDENSFIELD DOCTOR KILLED IN HOUSE FIRE

— Died Trying To Rescue Toddler

Aidensfield doctor Neil Bolton perished in a ferocious house fire on Wednesday evening while trying to rescue a toddler believed to have been trapped in an upstairs bedroom. Without any regard for his own safety, Dr. Bolton dived into the flames, tragically unaware that the boy had already been rescued by his stepbrother.

The fire broke out at around 8.50pm at 5 Green End Terrace, Aidensfield, where local writer Archie Roberts lived with his wife Stella, their two-year-old son Rupert and 15-year-old Julian Stephens, a son by Mrs. Roberts' first marriage. The blaze is thought to have started at a lean-to adjoining the house.

PARENTS ABSENT FROM SCENE

At the time Mr. Roberts was directing the Aidensfield Players' latest production at the village hall. Mrs. Roberts had returned home early with Rupert who was feeling unwell. She then left Julian to babysit while she went to a neighbour's house to telephone Dr. Bolton.

Alerted by shouts of 'Fire!', Mrs. Roberts emerged to see the lean-to engulfed in flames which were spreading to the house itself. On reaching the house, Mrs. Roberts, frantic with worry that little Rupert was trapped in his bedroom, opened the front door and the sudden inrush of oxygen caused the fire to rage ever more violently. Dr. Bolton arrived at the same time and pulled her back from the flames.

BRAVE DOCTOR SEARCHES

He removed his jacket, threw it over his head as protection and plunged into the inferno in search of the upstairs bedroom.
(continued on page 2)

P.C. Mike Bradley made two brave attempts to enter the burning house.

FIRE TRAGEDY

The last farewell: Dr. Neil Bolton sees wife Maggie off on holiday at Aidensfield station. Then tragedy struck.

(continued from page 1)

Mr. Roberts and P.C. Mike Bradley quickly arrived on the scene and were told that Dr. Bolton had gone into the burning house. A ladder was fetched and placed against the window of the upstairs bedroom. P.C. Bradley began to climb but as he neared the window, he was forced back by a sudden explosion which blew out the pane of glass.

BOY SAFE

But there was relief at ground level when Julian appeared holding his young stepbrother. He had brought the boy to safety via the back door.

With no sign of Dr. Bolton, P.C. Bradley bravely made another attempt to get into the house but the entire interior structure collapsed and he was again driven back by the heat.

At 9.03pm, officers from Ashfordly Fire Brigade began tackling the blaze. They eventually managed to force their way into the house where they found the body of Dr. Bolton on the ground floor. It is thought that he had reached the top of the stairs which then gave way beneath him.

Leading Fireman Roger Smedley said: 'By the time we arrived, the fire was burning fiercely. It took us three hours to bring it under control. There was no hope of being able to rescue Dr. Bolton.'

DANGEROUS PRACTICE

Thirty-six-year-old Dr. Bolton has been Aidensfield's G.P. for the past year and is the third incumbent of the post to die in the past three and a half years. The estranged husband of District Nurse Maggie Bolton, he came to the area in the spring of 1968 to work at Ashfordly Hospital before becoming the village doctor. He and Mrs. Bolton have recently been reconciled. She is currently away on holiday and is believed to be unaware of her husband's death.

The police were last night investigating any links between the fatal fire and recent blazes at Aidensfield Post Office and Half Mile Farm.

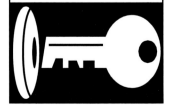
THE WORLD ABOUT US

- Neil Armstrong, commander of Apollo 11, became the first man to set foot on the moon.

- Senator Edward Kennedy pleaded guilty to leaving the scene of an accident after Mary Jo Kopechne, a passenger in his car, drowned near a bridge on Chappaquiddick Island, New England.

- Fresh from their free concert in Hyde Park, the Rolling Stones reached number one in the Hit Parade with 'Honky Tonk Women'.

MAN CONFESSES TO STARTING DEATH FIRE

Burnt Own House For Insurance —

Archibald Roberts, 44, has admitted starting the fire at his house which killed Aidensfield doctor Neil Bolton, Ashfordly Police revealed this week.

Dr. Bolton died in the fire at 5 Green End Terrace, Aidensfield, last Wednesday as he tried to rescue Roberts' two-year-old son from an upstairs bedroom. The boy was carried to safety by his stepbrother, Julian Stephens.

Police linked the fire to two earlier arson attacks — on a dustbin at Aidensfield Post Office and on a hayrick at Half Mile Farm. Traces of petrol were identified in a milk bottle found at the scene of the farm blaze.

YOUTHS INVOLVED

Local youth Trevor Chivers, who had been seen hanging around the hayrick shortly beforehand, was questioned about the incident and admitted that he and Julian Stephens were responsible for that fire as well as the one at the Post Office.

However Trevor Chivers had a cast-iron alibi for the time of the fatal fire — he was at the Village Hall rehearsing a play with P.C. Mike Bradley — and so Julian Stephens was interrogated alone. He denied any involvement but still faced a possible charge of murder.

The police began looking into the family background. Roberts and his wife Stella had moved from Leeds after he had lost his job and now he was struggling to earn a living as a writer. Sgt. Raymond Craddock learned that a few hours before the fire Roberts had moved essential items — the tools of his trade — from

The widowed Maggie Bolton is comforted on her return to Aidensfield by P.C. Mike Bradley.

his makeshift study into an old railway carriage half a mile away.

Considering this to be highly suspicious, Sgt. Craddock interviewed Roberts who, on hearing that his stepson could be facing a murder charge, confessed to setting fire to his house so that he could claim on the insurance. He had thought the house was empty, not realising that his young son had been brought home early because he was feeling poorly.

IN THE DOCK

Roberts was charged with manslaughter yesterday afternoon and will appear before Ashfordly Magistrates on Monday.

Mrs. Bolton did not know of her husband's death until returning from a short holiday on Tuesday. Friends of the couple say she is pregnant.

EX-WIFE BEHIND RESTAURANT VENDETTA

Builder Sidney Wainwright hits out at Alan Jackson.

The former wife of an Aidensfield restaurateur has been unmasked as the person behind a hate campaign directed at the business.

The vendetta against the Brass Lantern Restaurant on Aidensfield Green began last Thursday night, on the eve of the scheduled opening, when a brick was hurled through the window. The owners, listed as brothers Alan and Dennis Jackson, were then the victims of a practical joke on their opening night when diners presented them with bogus vouchers for free meals.

NEIGHBOURS

Police inquiries led them to local builder Sidney Wainwright who remained bitter after being outbid for the restaurant. On Saturday morning Wainwright even physically attacked Alan Jackson and was taken into custody where he admitted smashing the window but denied responsibility for the bogus coupons.

Two nights later, a slogan saying 'Condemned' was painted on the restaurant. This was followed by a threatening letter sent to Alan Jackson.

JACKSON FAMILY

Although the Jacksons told the police they did not want the matter pursued, officers questioned local printers in a bid to trace the source of the coupons. Johnson's Printers of Ashfordly said that they had printed them and that the order had come from a woman calling herself Debbie Rees.

(continued on page 6)

THE WORLD ABOUT US

– Sharon Tate, actress wife of film director Roman Polanski, was brutally murdered with four others at the couple's mansion in Beverly Hills, in the USA.

– 112 people were treated in hospital in Londonderry, Northern Ireland after another night of rioting.

– The has BBC announced its autumn programmes. Among them is a new comedy show with the curious title of *Monty Python's Flying Circus*.

WIFE'S VENDETTA

Sgt. Raymond Craddock, off duty, enjoys a meal at the Brass Lantern Restaurant.

(continued from page 5)

From letters in her room, P.C. Mike Bradley discovered that Debbie Rees's married name was Debbie Jackson and that her ex-husband was Alan Jackson. Pressed further by the police, Alan Jackson finally admitted that he and Dennis are not brothers but are a couple. His ex-wife had apparently wanted to wreck his new life with Dennis to repay him for ruining their marriage.

Sgt. Raymond Craddock of Ashfordly Police commented:

'It is a most unusual case and since neither of the gentlemen wish to press charges, there is nothing more we can do.'

STRANGE FRUIT

One villager who did not wish to be named said: 'It's just not natural two men living together like that. Whatever's the world coming to? You certainly wouldn't catch me setting foot in their restaurant now I know what they get up to.'

Yesterday morning a 'For Sale' sign appeared outside the Willow.

SGT. RAYMOND CRADDOCK — AN APOLOGY

In last week's *Gazette* we carried a story which referred to the possibility that a button found on waste ground may have come from the uniform of Sgt. Raymond Craddock of Ashfordly Police. We now realise that Sgt.

Craddock would never be seen on duty with a button missing nor would he ever venture out in public in a less than immaculate state of attire. Therefore we apologise unreservedly for any distress caused.

PIGS ON RAMPAGE

Fifteen squealing piglets caused chaos in the centre of Aidensfield on Monday when they escaped from their pen and ran amok. As villagers joined forces to round up the strays, one piglet was found in the Smoke Room at the Aidensfield Arms while another had a close encounter with the bacon slicer at Aidensfield Stores.

PIG SEARCH

Eventually all were rounded up bar one. The missing piglet is described as 'pink, with a snub nose and a curly tail'.

The animals had recently been bought at auction by local livestock expert Claude Jeremiah Greengrass. 'I was meant to be buying sheep for a customer but my assistant David went and bid for the piglets in my name,' said an irate Mr. Greengrass. 'That's the trouble with that lad, he's just too soft — particularly in the head.'

MAN'S BURIAL RUINED BY FLOOD

— 'Grave Error' Says Funeral Director

The funeral of 76-year-old Samuel Hawkins at Aidensfield Church on Wednesday afternoon degenerated into black comedy when his grave suddenly filled with water during the burial.

The flooding, thought to have been caused by the removal of lead piping in the vicinity, angered mourners. The deceased's widow May later remarked caustically: 'If I'd wanted him buried at sea, I'd have hired a ruddy boat.'

LAST DISRESPECTS

Some 20 mourners had gathered in the churchyard to pay their last respects to Mr. Hawkins, an ex-farmer who had lived in the district all his life. Following a solemn and moving service and an address from the vicar, the Rev. Arnold Peabody, the coffin was just about to be lowered into the grave when one of the gathering noticed that water was seeping into the burial area.

Within a matter of minutes, the water in the grave rose alarmingly to a level of two feet. As pandemonium broke out and mourners scattered, the burial was abandoned. The coffin was returned to a place of rest inside the church until the leak could be repaired.

BITTER

Funeral director Bernie Scripps said: 'It's the first time anything like that has ever happened to me. It was a shame really.'

The wake, scheduled for the deceased's house at Croft Terrace, Aidensfield, was also postponed, prompting a stinging rebuke from Mrs. Hawkins.

(continued on page 10)

THE WORLD ABOUT US

- Former world heavyweight boxing champion Rocky Marciano died in a plane crash.

- North Vietnamese President Ho Chi Minh died from a heart attack.

- Australian business tycoon Rupert Murdoch pressed ahead with his bid to buy the *Sun* newspaper.

- Bob Dylan topped the bill at the second Isle of Wight Festival of Music before a crowd of 150,000 who paid £2 10s each for the privilege.

FLOODED GRAVE

Mourners at the Hawkins' funeral pictured moments before the unexpected flood.

(continued from page 9)

'I'd been up all night buttering sandwiches,' she raged, 'and that's two jars of fish paste gone to waste.'

The vicar was equally unforgiving. 'I am determined to get to the bottom of this unfortunate business,' he said. 'All I know is that last week I hired a local gardener, Claude Jeremiah Greengrass, to dig over a patch of wasteland so that it could be used as an extension for the church graveyard. I have not been able to speak to Mr. Greengrass yet but I am led to understand that he and his young assistant, David Stockwell, unearthed some old lead pipes which Mr. Greengrass then tried to sell to a lady of his acquaintance as part of a heating system.

'I gather that when the lady in question learned that the pipes came from the churchyard, she did not want them in the house. I understand from Mr. Scripps that on Tuesday he asked Mr. Greengrass to prepare a grave for Mr. Hawkins' burial. It would appear that the removal of the pipes by Mr. Greengrass and his subsequent failure to replace them led to the underground flooding. I shall be very interested to hear his version of events.'

Yesterday the door at Mr. Greengrass' smallholding was answered by the young David Stockwell who, when asked about his employer's whereabouts, said: 'You're not here, are you, Mr. Greengrass?'

HECKLER EJECTED

A ten-year-old boy was ejected from the audience at Aidensfield Players' production of 'Julius Caesar' in the Village Hall on Tuesday. The eviction followed complaints from cast members that he had shouted out 'He's behind you' just as Brutus prepared to stab Caesar in the back.

The Players' new artistic director Felix Hamshaw said: 'The outburst ruined the entire performance. My actors' nerves are ripped to shreds. That's what comes of too much pantomime.'

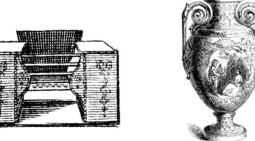

HEARTBEAT EPISODE LIST

SERIES ONE

1. Changing Places by Johnny Byrne
2. Fruits of the Earth by Johnny Byrne
3. Rumours by David Lane
4. Playing With Fire by Rob Gittins
5. Nowt But a Prank by Barry Woodward
6. Old, New, Borrowed and Blue by Alan Whiting
7. Face Value by David Lane
8. Outsiders by Peter Barwood
9. Primal Instinct by Brian Finch
10. Keep On Running by Johnny Byrne

SERIES TWO

11. Secrets by Adele Rose
12. End of the Line by David Martin
13. Manhunt by David Lane
14. Bitter Harvest by Jane Hollowood
15. Over the Hill by Johnny Byrne
16. Bang to Rights by Brian Finch
17. A Talent For Deception by Jonathan Critchley
18. Baby Blues by Veronica Henry
19. Wall of Silence by Jane Hollowood
20. Missing by Adele Rose

SERIES THREE

21. Speed Kills by David Martin
22. Riders of the Storm by Brian Finch
23. Dead Ringer by Johnny Byrne
24. Going Home by Johnny Byrne
25. A Chilly Reception by Eric Wendell
26. The Frighteners by Brian Finch
27. Father's Day by Brian Finch
28. Endangered Species by Michael Russell
29. An American in Aidensfield by Peter Palliser
30. Bringing it All Back Home by Michael Russell

The rarely-seen Whitby Lifeboat.

SERIES FOUR

31. Wild Thing by Michael Russell
32. Witch Hunt by Brian Finch
33. Mid Day Sun by Jonathan Critchley
34. Turn of the Tide by Johnny Byrne
35. Love Child by Brian Finch
36. Nice Girls Don't by Jane Hollowood
37. Trouble in Mind by Johnny Byrne
38. Fair Game by Veronica Henry
39. Red Herring by Michael Russell
40. Arms and the Man by Jonathan Critchley
41. Treading Carefully by Lizzie Mickery
42. Bad Blood by Steve Trafford
43. Assault and Battery by Freda Kelsall
44. Lost and Found by Johnny Byrne
45. A Bird in the Hand… by Jonathan Critchley and Peter N Walker
46. A Winter's Tale by Brian Finch

SERIES FIVE

47. Wishing Well by Johnny Byrne
48. Expectations by Lizzie Mickery
49. Thief in the Night by Jane Hollowood
50. Domestic by Brian Finch
51. Vacant Possession by John Stevenson
52. We're All Allies Really by Peter Tinniswood
53. Sophie's Choice by Rob Gittins
54. Gone Tomorrow by Freda Kelsall
55. Toss Up by James Robson
56. It's All in the Game by Ron Rose
57. Vigilante by Brian Finch
58. Unfinished Business by Jane Hollowood
59. Saint Columba's Treasure by Jonathan Critchley
60. Sitting Off the Dock of the Bay by Rob Gittins
61. Blood Sports by Brian Finch

Everyone's favourite dog, Alfred (right) with his owner, Claude Jeremiah Greengrass.

SERIES SIX

62. Kids by Brian Finch
63. Old Colonials by Ron Rose
64. Forget Me Not by Jane Hollowood
65. A Long Shot by David Lane
66. Something of Value by Johnny Byrne
67. Frail Mortality by Keith Temple
68. Snapped by Peter Gibbs
69. Catch Us If You Can by Brian Finch
70. Giving the Game Away by Guy Meredith
71. The Championship by Jane Hollowood
72. Who Needs Enemies by Brian Finch
73. Thanks to Alfred by Rob Gittins
74. Obsessions by Peter Gibbs
75. The Best Laid Plans by Freda Kelsall
76. Bygones Be Bygones by Peter Gibbs
77. Old Friends by Ron Rose
78. Charity Begins at Home by Jane Hollowood

Alfred in the snow.

Jo Weston.

Ruby & Jo.

Greengrass helping the community.

SERIES SEVEN

79. Bad Apple by Peter Gibbs
80. Pig in the Middle by Brian Finch
81. Small Beer by Bill Lyons
82. Closing Ranks by Jane Hollowood
83. Leaving Home by David Lane
84. Fool For Love by James Stevenson
85. The Family Way by Brian Finch
86. Friendly Fire by Peter Gibbs
87. Sons and Lovers by Susan Wilkins
88. Playing With Trains by James Stevenson
89. What the Butler Saw by Garry Lyons
90. Affairs of the Heart by Jane Hollowood
91. Peace and Quiet by Peter Barwood
92. Substitutes by Ron Rose
93. In on the Act by Veronica Henry
94. The Queen's Message by Peter Gibbs
95. Brainstorm by Peter Barwood
96. Bad Penny by Peter Barwood
97. Appearances by Carolyn Sally Jones
98. Local Knowledge by Brian Finch
99. The Enemy Within by Susan Wilkins
100. Unconsidered Trifles by Jonathan Critchley
101. Heroes and Villains by Peter Gibbs
102. Love Me Do by Jane Hollowood

SERIES EIGHT

Three men and a baby: Blaketon, Bellamy, Ventress and friend.

District Nurse Maggie Bolton.

PRINCIPAL CAST LIST

P.C. Mike Bradley . . . . Jason Durr

P.C. Nick Rowan . . . . Nick Berry

Dr. Kate Rowan . . . . Niamh Cusack

Claude Jeremiah Greengrass . . . . Bill Maynard

Oscar Blaketon . . . . Derek Fowlds

P.C. Alf Ventress . . . . William Simons

P.C. Phil Bellamy . . . . Mark Jordan

Gina Ward . . . . Tricia Penrose

Maggie Bolton . . . . Kazia Pelka

Jo Weston . . . . Juliette Gruber

Sgt. Raymond Craddock . . . . Philip Franks

George Ward . . . . Stuart Golland

Aunt Eileen . . . . Anne Stallybrass

Dr. Alex Ferrenby . . . . Frank Middlemass

Bernie Scripps . . . . Peter Benson

David Stockwell . . . . David Lonsdale

Jackie Lambert . . . . Fiona Dolman

Dr. Neil Bolton . . . . David Michaels

Auntie Mary . . . . Arbel Jones

Sue Driscoll . . . . Keeley Forsyth

ACKNOWLEDGEMENTS

The author would like to thank the following for their help in the preparation of this book: Keith Richardson, Gerry Mill, Pat Brown, Bill Maynard, Jason Durr, Derek Fowlds, William Simons, Mark Jordan, Philip Franks, Tricia Penrose, Kazia Pelka, Peter Benson, David Lonsdale, Fiona Dolman, Teresa Ferlinc, Martin Curry, Addie Orfila, Karen Jensen, Kathryn de Belle and Susanna Wadeson plus Julian Flanders, Roland Hall, Katya Sommer and Carole McDonald at Design/Section and Nicky Paris at André Deutsch.